OSPREY COMBAT AIRCRAFT • 30

US NAVY
F-4 PHANTOM II
MiG KILLERS
1972-73

SERIES EDITOR: TONY HOLMES

OSPREY COMBAT AIRCRAFT • 30

US NAVY F-4 PHANTOM II MiG KILLERS 1972-73

Brad Elward and Peter Davies

OSPREY
PUBLISHING

First published in Great Britain in 2002 by Osprey Publishing,
Midland House, West Way, Botley, Oxford OX2 0PH, UK
44-02 23rd St, Suite 219, Long Island City, NY 11101, USA
E-mail: info@ospreypublishing.com

Transferred to digital print on demand 2009

First published 2002
2nd impression 2008

Printed and bound by PrintOnDemand-Worldwide.com Peterborough, UK

A CIP catalogue record for this book is available from the British Library

ISBN: 978 1 84176 264 7

Editorial and photo captions by Tony Holmes
Page design by Mark Holt
Cover artwork by Iain Wyllie
Aircraft profiles by Jim Laurier
Cartography by Zaur Eylanbekov
Origination by Grasmere Digital Imaging, Leeds, UK
Typeset in Adobe Garamond, Rockwell and Univers

Editor's note

To make this best-selling series as authoritative as possible, the Editor would be interested in hearing from any individual who may have relevant
photographs, documentation or first-hand experiences relating to the world's combat aircraft, and the crews that flew them, in the various theatres of war.
Any material used will be credited to its original source. Please write to Tony Holmes at 16 Sandilands, Chipstead, Sevenoaks, Kent, TN13 2SP or send
an e-mail to tony.holmes@zen.co.uk.

Acknowledgements

The Editor wishes to thank the following individuals for their valuable photographic contributions – Robert F Dorr, Capt John C Ensch (Ret.) and his
squadronmates at VF-161, Michael France, Capt Jerry Houston (Ret.), Dave Menard, Peter Mersky, Michael Padgett, Angelo Romano and Nick Stroud.
The authors and Editor acknowledge the contribution made by Tom Chee and Alan Howarth, who provided much of the material included within the
Colour Plates commentaries. Finally, thanks to Adm Winston 'Cope' Copeland (Ret.) for explaining why he was 'in hack' in June 1972.

Front Cover

On the afternoon of 6 March 1972, VF-111 'Sundowners' became the first fighter unit within the US Navy to claim MiG kills with two different
types of aircraft. Lt Garry L 'Greyhound' Weigand and Lt(jg) William C 'Farkle' Freckleton (in F-4B BuNo 153019) destroyed a MiG-17 during a
FORCAP mission in support of photo-reconnaissance assets sent to overfly Wuang Lang airfield. This victory was claimed three-and-a-half
years after 'Sundowner' Lt Tony Nargi had bagged a MiG-21 in an F-8C on 19 September 1968. The unit's first, and only, F-4 MiG kill did not
come easy, for the North Vietnamese jet was flown both aggressively and skilfully by its pilot. However, outnumbered two to one, the
communist pilot was eventually downed thanks to the employment of superior tactics by the two VF-111 crews. The final moments of the action
were related by Lt Weigand in his post-mission encounter report;

'I pulled my nose onto the MiG just as he hit the 'burner. Jim (Lt Jim 'Yosemite' Stillinger, who was Weigand's flight leader) came up with "Do
you have the MiG?" I rogered that I had him. He said "Shoot! Shoot! Shoot!". I was at 480 ft, looking down about 50 ft to the MiG as I squeezed
the trigger. After what seemed like hours, the missile came off, did a couple of zig-zags and flew right up his tailpipe. I figured we were about
three-quarters of a mile behind him at dead six.

'The instant that I squeezed the trigger everything went into slow motion. I saw the missile disappear into the tailpipe of the camouflaged MiG
but nothing seemed to happen right away. I was just about to fire another missile when a big piece of debris flew up into the airstream behind
the MiG. Then suddenly his whole tail came off, tumbling end over end, and a tremendous gout of black smoke erupted from him. He started
into a glide for the ground. I figured I had better check my six, since it had been a long time. I pulled hard right, reversed left, and by that time
the MiG had hit the ground. Jim watched him go all the way in, exploding on a hillside. The MiG driver did not eject, probably because he was
incapacitated.' (*Cover artwork by Iain Wyllie*)

FOR A CATALOGUE OF ALL BOOKS PUBLISHED BY
OSPREY MILITARY AND AVIATION PLEASE CONTACT:

Osprey Direct, c/o Random House Distribution Center,
400 Hahn Road, Westminster, MD 21157
Email: uscustomerservice@ospreypublishing.com

Osprey Direct, The Book Service Ltd, Distribution Centre,
Colchester Road, Frating Green, Colchester, Essex, CO7 7DW
E-mail: customerservice@ospreypublishing.com

www.ospreypublishing.com

CONTENTS

RISING TENSIONS

By the first weeks of 1972, American aircraft had been conducting 'reprisal' raids against targets in North Vietnam – called 'protective reactive' strikes – for a number of months. These missions usually followed North Vietnamese attempts to attack US aeroplanes flying *Blue Tree* reconnaissance sorties. These reprisal raids were the first strike missions to be flown against North Vietnam since the end of the *Rolling Thunder* campaign in October 1968.

Under the Rules of Engagement (ROE) then in place, if a reconnaissance aircraft was fired on, the crews were prohibited from calling back to the carrier for strikes to hit the offending AAA or SAM site. However, if the strike aeroplanes were actually flying with the recce package when it came under fire, they could execute 'protective reaction strikes'.

While at first these 'strikes' were defensive in nature, being aimed at the air defence batteries that fired on the American aircraft, they soon became larger operations against specific targets such as fuel storage facilities and MiG bases, complete with strike, flak suppression and CAP sections.

Although the MiGs had not been active in the latter months of 1971, some did stage out of Kep, Phuc Yen, Yen Bai and Quan Lang, using heavy Ground Control Intercept (GCI) radar control. Communist pilots would occasionally try to lure US air forces into anti-aircraft artillery (AAA) and surface-to-air missile (SAM) traps by flying low through site fields-of-fire (which would be the case on 10 May 1972).

On 19 January 1972, two F-4Js on MiGCAP engaged VPAF jets for the first time since March 1970. The Phantom IIs were from VF-96, and they had launched in support of a 19-aeroplane Alpha strike sortied by Carrier Air Wing Nine (CVW-9) from USS *Constellation* (CVA-64). The F-4s were crewed by Lt Randall H 'Duke' Cunningham and Lt(jg) William 'Willie' P Driscoll (in BuNo 157267, call sign 'Showtime 112') and Lts Brian 'Bulldog' Grant and Jerry Sullivan.

The strike was a protective reaction sortie in retaliation for the downing of a CVW-9 A-6A Intruder (from VA-165) by a SAM on 30 December 1971. This aircraft was participating in a five-day aerial campaign called Operation *Proud Deep Alpha*, which was intended to destroy the stockpiles of weapons and supplies that North Vietnam was assembling near the Demilitarized Zone. VF-111, flying off the USS *Coral Sea* (CVA-43), had also lost an F-4B to a SAM that same day.

In the early afternoon of 19 January 1972, Lt Randall 'Duke' Cunningham and Lt(jg) William 'Willie' Driscoll of VF-96 downed a MiG-21 with an AIM-9 missile. This was the first aerial kill claimed by an American aircraft in 22 months, and to prove that it was no fluke, Cunningham and Driscoll went on to down a further four MiGs over the next four months to become the only Navy aces of the Vietnam war. This photograph was taken at NAS Miramar on 5 October 1972, three months after the completion of VF-96's penultimate wartime *WestPac*. Note the five MiG-17 silhouettes, in red, painted on the crews' 'bone domes', and the red VPAF kill markings on the splitter plate behind Cunningham's right leg (*via Peter Mersky*)

Returning to 19 January, *Constellation*'s Alpha strike was tasked with attacking caves suspected of housing MiGs, as well as three SAM sites. All were located in the Quan Lang area.

According to 'Duke' Cunningham, the strike force was briefed to expect SAMs en route to the target area, and a long egress had been planned to bypass this threat. 'We were told that we would encounter AAA, SAMs and MiGs in the target area. Two MiG-21s were known to be operating out of Quan Lang field and six were based at Bai Thuong, about 60 miles to the north.'

The entire strike force departed the ship (only the F-4s refuelled

Although of indifferent quality, this rare photograph more than qualifies for inclusion in this volume by dint of the fact that it shows 'Randy' Cunningham and 'Willie' Driscoll at the controls of 'Showtime 112', which was their 'MiG-killing' jet of 19 January. Indeed, this shot was taken just days prior to them claiming their MiG-21 (*via Peter Mersky*)

immediately after take-off) and ingressed to a point 45 nautical miles south-west of Quan Lang (designated as Point Alpha). To help conceal their intent, the package flew over northern South Vietnam, turned north and flew up into Laos until opposite Quan Lang, then flew back east to the target. To conserve fuel, maximum range cruise profiles of 20,000-22,000 ft altitude and 310 knots were flown.

A flight of three Shrike anti-radiation missile-equipped A-7E Corsair IIs (dubbed 'Iron Hand') and two F-4 flak suppression aircraft led the force, followed by the main package of A-6A and A-7E attack jets trailing to the left and right, respectively. A solitary RA-5C Vigilante photo-recce aircraft and its F-4 escort flew above and behind the Alpha package, while the MiGCAP (Cunningham/Driscoll and Grant/Sullivan) trailed the recce jet. Finally, an A-3 ECM/tanker and KA-6 tanker remained behind the formation in support.

The photo Vigilante drew fire upon reaching Point Alpha, so the A-7 'Iron Hand' and F-4 flak suppression aircraft turned right and started their run into the target, while the remainder of the force continued on course toward a point 30 nautical miles south-east of Quan Lang (called Point Bravo). There, the two strike divisions and the MiGCAP turned in an easterly direction towards the target, while the RA-5 and its escort continued on course north. The two tankers then established an orbit.

According to aircrews participating in this mission, the intent was to confuse the enemy as much as possible by having the aircraft converge on the target from several different angles.

As the strike divisions turned towards Point Bravo, Cunningham and Driscoll, and their wing (Grant and Sullivan, on their left, line-abreast, about one nautical mile away) started a slow, descending turn to approach the target slightly north of the strike track. Cunningham later said that he intended to pass just north of the airfield and establish an orbit point about 20 nautical miles north-east of Quan Lang, between the target area and the MiG base at Bai Thuong. His idea was to position the MiGCAP to intercept any jets launching from Bai Thuong, but at about 15 nautical miles west of Quan Lang, he started picking up height-finder and AAA radar on his Radar-Homing and Warning (RHAW) gear, and he could see the southern group taking heavy 23 and 37 mm groundfire. According to Cunningham, this route had been a mistake, as they were smack in the middle of two SAM sites.

The lead VF-96 jet was at 17,000 ft, flying at 500 knots north-west of the field, when Cunningham received positive SAM-launch indications, and he saw a missile rising from the northern site. 'The missile was coming right up under Grant's belly – he couldn't see it. I called, "Break left", but he didn't break hard enough, so I called for a harder break'. The missile passed about ten feet from Grant's canopy and detonated high at 20,000-25,000 ft. Cunningham later suggested that the missile must have been defective because the proximity fuse warhead fitted to the SA-2 was effective up to a distance of 350 ft.

He then received further RHAW warnings that the southern SAM site (at his 'two o'clock') had him locked-up. Cunningham reversed to the right and saw a SAM launch. 'I could see a little white glow and the dust flying'. Still at about 17,000 ft, he and his wingman broke right and down. 'This one kept tracking – I wasn't defeating it. So, I rolled inverted, waited until the missile was within half a mile of us, then pulled hard into a split-S type manoeuvre. I put the stick in my lap and pulled about 9G'. The missile sailed harmlessly by and exploded about 1000 ft high.

Cunningham recovered and headed north-west at a height of 10,000 ft and 300 knots. He immediately saw another SAM launched at him from the northern site. 'The F-4 can pull only about 3-4G at 300 knots, so I engaged "burner". I still had the tank, so I unloaded. I was hanging in the straps. I rolled into the missile, and as it approached me, I buried the stick in my lap'. The SAM detonated in the immediate vicinity of the Phantom II, flipping it from about a 135-degree nose low, left bank to about a 45-degree right bank, nose high, but remarkably caused no damage.

While trying to regain altitude, Cunningham looked down and saw what he believed to be two A-7s at his 'one o'clock', three nautical miles away, heading north through a canyon at a height of 500 ft. 'As I was looking around for more SAMs, although I wasn't having any RHAW indications, it dawned on me that those two birds were in afterburner, and the A-7 doesn't have a 'burner! I looked back at them and started my nose down, still in 'burner'.

Indeed, Cunningham's 'A-7s' were actually two silver MiG-21s. The fighter on the left was flying at about 500 ft, while the second MiG was abeam to the right in a fighting wing, stepped up a further 300-500 ft above his leader. Cunningham made the call, 'Bandits! Blue Bandits! North of the field!' Descending rapidly to about 200 ft, he accelerated to 500 knots and closed on the lead MiG from behind.

'I thought about punching off my centreline tank, but at that airspeed in the F-4 we were having problems with it hitting the stabilator – at that altitude I didn't want any control problems. I told my RIO (Radar Intercept Officer, Lt(jg) Driscoll) that the pipper was on him – he hit the boresight switch and called "Locked-on, 50 knots closing – shoot, shoot, shoot your Sparrow". I reached over and hit the "heat" switch. It didn't make my RIO very happy, but from the tail aspect I was much more confident with the Sidewinder than I was with the Sparrow.'

Cunningham (now at 300 ft, and speeding over the jungle at 500 knots) launched one AIM-9G at the lead MiG from 'six o'clock' at a distance of about two miles, calling 'Fox Two!' He said that neither MiG appeared to have seen him until his missile launched, at which point the lead MiG broke hard to the right. He believes that the second MiG must have called a 'break', because his victim couldn't have seen the Sidewinder. From a 'six o'clock', tailpipe position at the time of missile launch, the next thing Cunningham saw was a plan view of the lead MiG 'really hauling, still in after-

Cunningham and Driscoll's five kills were claimed using these two machines, 'Showtime 112' (BuNo 157267) and 'Showtime 100' (BuNo 155800). Both jets had served with VF-96 for some time prior to them 'bagging' five of the eight MiGs credited to the unit in 1972, BuNo 157267 joining from VF-121 on 2 February 1971 and BuNo 155800 arriving fresh from McDonnell Douglas's St Louis plant on 19 October 1968. This photograph was taken soon after the squadron commenced operations from *Yankee Station* in November 1971 (*via Angelo Romano*)

burner'. The AIM-9 missed and impacted the ground. 'They must have been H or J-model MiGs', Cunningham later explained, 'as the MiG-21 just can't turn that fast without hydraulically-boosted controls'.

Expecting the MiG to continue its turn into him, Cunningham pulled up into a high speed 'yo-yo' and made a 'baby barrel roll' to the left to maintain position. 'I expected the big cross-turn – they were trying to bring me right down between them. Instead, his wingman just left him – he pushed over and ran.'

After Cunningham's first weapon missed its mark, the lead MiG reversed its turn and continued towards Bai Thuong. 'A lot of my BQM (drone) training went through my mind as I engaged that MiG – my overtake, altitude and airspeed. And when he reversed, it was just like I'd called for the BQM to reverse', Cunningham remembers.

The MiG's reversal repositioned it directly in front of 'Showtime 112', and from less than a mile away, Cunningham triggered a second AIM-9, which went directly up the jet's tailpipe. The aft section of the MiG appeared to come off, the nose tucked down violently, and the aircraft hit the ground, tumbling head-over-tail – no 'chute was seen. As Cunningham quickly turned right to avoid ingesting debris, he saw the second MiG at '12 o'clock', about two-and-half nautical miles away, fleeing the area.

The MiG had pushed over in an acceleration manoeuvre and was heading north-west, starting to pull away. Cunningham was now at 450 knots, still in afterburner, and carrying his centreline tank as he started pursuit. He chased the second MiG for about 30 nautical miles, with the communist jet slightly increasing the separation distance. The MiG pilot then started to climb, and Cunningham began to close on him. 'I was going to chase him right to Bai Thuong but my RIO asked me for our (fuel) state. I said, "Willie, don't bother me know. I'm chasing a MiG", and he replied, "No shit. I want your state RIGHT NOW!" I glanced at it and was astounded to see that we were down to 6500 lbs – when using the afterburner, fuel just went like that. We now barely had enough to exit through the SAMs to a tanker'.

By this time Cunningham and Driscoll (who were flying at tree-top height) were taking ground fire from both sides, and could see tracers

'Showtime 112' traps back aboard the *Constellation* at the end of its historic 'MiG killing' mission on the afternoon of 19 January 1972. And despite the adrenaline coursing through 'Randy' Cunningham's body after he had downed the Navy's first MiG in almost two years, he still looks set to snag a three-wire on landing! After service with VF-96, BuNo 157267 briefly rejoined Pacific Fleet Replacement Air Group (RAG) squadron VF-121, before moving to VF-114 on 19 December 1972. It remained with the 'Aardvarks' until 28 April 1975, completing a further two *WestPac* deployments (aboard *Kitty Hawk*) in this period. Serving with VF-121 for the last time between May 1975 and May 1976, BuNo 157267 then joined VF-21. It remained in the frontline with the 'Freelancers' until September 1977 (and completed a solitary *WestPac* aboard the *Ranger*), when the jet was transferred to MCAS Kaneohe Bay-based VMFA-232. BuNo 157267 was flown by this unit in Hawaii and Japan (MCAS Iwakuni) until issued to fellow Kaneohe Bay resident VMFA-235 in March 1979. Sent to the Naval Air Rework Facility (NARF) at NAS North Island, San Diego, in October of that same year, the fighter emerged from its overhaul on 15 July 1980 as an F-4S. BuNo 157267 was then sent to VMFA-122 at MCAS Beaufort, South Carolina, where it remained until retired to the Military Aircraft Storage and Disposition Center (MASDC) at Davis-Monthan AFB, Arizona, on 13 December 1984 – the F-4 had completed some 4354 flight hours by this time (*via P Mersky*)

passing over their canopy. However, they had a full system lock-on, and Cunningham felt compelled to try a desperation shot. Moreover, he knew that he was not going to catch the MiG for an AIM-9 shot. With his F-4 just 200 ft above the ground, he triggered off an AIM-7E-2 at the MiG, which was at 400 ft some three nautical miles away, and opening, in front of the Phantom II. The Sparrow failed to launch, however, and it was later discovered that there was a shorted cable that prevented the ejector cartridge from firing. Cunningham, with his wing still flying cover, then made a left climbing turn to 20,000 ft, egressed and headed for the tanker.

The RA-5 pilot had seen the lead MiG crash and attempted to photograph the scene, but was forced to abort because of SAMs. A total of 18 SA-2s were launched at the force but none inflicted any damage.

'Duke' Cunningham and 'Willie' Driscoll received a warm welcome once they got back to CVA-64. 'There was real elation among the 5000 people on the "Connie". It was the first kill in almost two years, and we had quite a welcoming committee. In fact, one of the enlisted men knocked the Admiral over to jump up on the aeroplane and grab my arm to say "Mr Cunningham, we got our MiG today, didn't we?!"'

According to the *Red Baron* intelligence report written up by the Navy after this engagement, 'the most significant comment we can make regarding this event is that the crews were well prepared mentally. They knew how to effectively employ their weapons and had the ability to manoeuvre their aircraft to the desired position. It is significant that they felt they had "been there before" because of their training with the ACM'.

Furthermore, Cunningham's backseater, 'Willie' Driscoll, had insisted on a fuel check during the engagement, which probably saved them from walking home.

Following this action, air activity slowed down for the next two months, although *Blue Tree* protective reaction strikes continued, permitting the Americans to stage the largest ongoing 'unofficial' campaign against North Vietnam since the cessation of *Rolling Thunder* in October 1968.

'SUNDOWNER' SUCCESS

The next Navy Phantom II MiG kill occurred during the afternoon of 6 March 1972, when a pair of F-4Bs from VF-111 'Sundowners' successfully manoeuvred a MiG-17 into a 'sandwich' for a kill.

The two jets from the *Coral Sea* had launched as a FORCAP (Force CAP) section in support of a photo-reconnaissance mission to Quan Lang airfield. FORCAP referred to fighters that were directed to a spot north of the carriers to intercept any MiGs that may attempt to attack the vessel. However, if a reconnaissance jet saw any 'bogies', the FORCAPs were cleared to intercept the enemy aircraft as they returned north.

Lt James 'Yosemite' Stillinger (a former F-8 Crusader pilot with a prior combat tour, and a recent Topgun graduate) and Lt(jg) Rick Olin crewed the lead Phantom II, while Lt Garry L Weigand and Lt(jg) William C Freckleton flew as their wing (in F-4B BuNo 153019, call-sign 'Old Nick 201').

Interestingly, Weigand and Freckleton had originally been scheduled to fly as wing for Lt Cdr Jim Ruliffson and his 'nugget' RIO, Lt(jg) Clark van Nostrand. Ruliffson (call-sign 'Cobra') was one of the founding members of Topgun, and he was well respected in the fleet for his tactical expertise. Indeed, his ability as a Phantom II pilot was legendary. But as the F-4s were holding on the catapults, Ruliffson's jet sprung a hydraulics leak and had to be scratched. 'He was livid', Bill Freckleton recalled.

Moustache-toting Stillinger and Olin, who were waiting on hot-fuel standby, were then moved onto the starboard catapult and assumed section lead. Both F-4s were experiencing radar problems (Olin had only pulse search and Bill Freckleton's radar was absolutely dead), which ruled out the employment of Sparrows should MiGs being engaged.

As with the 19 January photo-mission to Quan Lang, the crews conducting the reconnaissance flight on 6 March planned to use the 'back door' route into Laos, before flying back towards the target.

Quan Lang was one of many MiG airfields that had been extensively reinforced during the bombing halt following *Rolling Thunder*. When that campaign ended in October 1968, Quan Lang was home to some 150 MiGs, mostly MiG-17s. By 1972, the base had grown to accommodate some 260 fighters, 95 of which were MiG-21s and 30 Chinese-built MiG-19s. These jets were being regularly sortied by the VPAF to harass B-52 missions to Laos, and to provide cover for the build-up of supplies for the coming offensive against South Vietnam.

After launch, Stillinger and Weigand were vectored into the area by the *Red Crown* controller, who on this day was Senior Chief Radarman Larry Nowell aboard the cruiser USS *Chicago* (CG-11). The senior chief would

VF-111's sole F-4 'MiG killer' basks in the sun at NAS Miramar in August 1972. Note the MiG-17 silhouette on the jet's splitter plate. Accepted by the Navy at St Louis on 5 May 1966, this aircraft remained with McDonnell for research and development work until 29 July, when it was issued to VF-213. BuNo 153019 embarked with the unit on *Kitty Hawk* on 5 November for the 'Black Lions'' second (of six) *WestPacs*. It went on to complete a further two combat cruises with CVW-11/CVA-63 prior to its transfer to VF-121 on 29 December 1969. Remaining with the RAG until 17 March 1971, BuNo 153019 then joined VF-111 and participated in its fourth *WestPac*, aboard the *Coral Sea*. The jet completed a fifth combat cruise, again with VF-111, in 1973. Transitioning to the F-4N in mid-1974, the 'Sundowners' duly passed BuNo 153019 on to VMFA-531 at MCAS El Toro, California, in October. The jet was sent to NARF North Island in March 1975, where it remained in cocooned storage until converted into an N-model as part of Project *Beeline* between June and September 1976 – it was the 198th F-4B to be upgraded. BuNo 153019 was issued to reserve-manned VF-201 at NAS Dallas on 23 May 1977, and it continued to serve with the Texas-based unit until transferred to VF-171 at NAS Key West, Florida, on 10 February 1984. Stricken from the inventory two weeks later, BuNo 153019 has guarded the gate at the Florida naval air station since October 1984. It is the sole survivor of the 16 Navy F-4s to have claimed a kill during *Rolling Thunder* (*via Brad Elward*)

Four of the five key players involved in securing VF-111's MiG-17 kill (on the afternoon of 6 March 1972) pose for the ship's photographer in *Coral Sea's* hangar deck the day after the mission. They are, from left to right, Lt(jg) William 'Farkle' Freckleton ('Old Nick 201's' RIO), Senior Chief Radarman Larry Nowell (the 'ace' *Red Crown* fighter controller from the cruiser *Chicago*), Lt Garry 'Greyhound' Weigand (the pilot of 'Old Nick 201') and Lt James 'Yosemite' Stillinger (section leader on the 'MiG killing' mission) (*via Angelo Romano*)

'Old Nick 204' (BuNo 150466) and 'Screaming Eagle 113' (BuNo 149457) drop their standard low-drag Mk 82 500-lb bombs through broken cloud whilst flying over North Vietnam at medium level in March 1972. Note how the aircrafts' Triple Ejector Racks (TERs) are secured to the underside of the twin Sidewinder mounting. This photograph was taken just 48 hours after Garry Weigand and Bill Freckleton had destroyed their MiG-17. Three months later, on 11 June, 'Screaming Eagle 113' got in on the action when its crew downed CVW-15's fifth, and final, MiG of the air wing's highly eventful 1971-72 *WestPac* deployment (*via Aerospace Publishing*)

subsequently be involved in no less than 13 successful MiG-killing sorties, and was awarded a Distinguished Service Medal on 17 August 1972 for his efforts, becoming only the second Navy enlisted man so honoured.

Once in communication with the VF-111 crews, Nowell directed them to establish an orbit on-station above Brandon Bay. As soon as they arrived, they heard the photo jet call 'Bandits! Bandits! Two Blue Bandits!', indicating MiG-21s, then, 'More! Red bandits! Red bandits! Two, no I think I see three Red Bandits!', indicating the presence of the more nimble MiG-17s. At this point, the MiGCAP, which had been orbiting in Laos (two F-4Bs from VF-111's sister unit, VF-51, crewed by squadron CO Cdr Foster S 'Tooter' Teague and RIO Lt Ralph M Howell, and Ops Officer Lt Cdr Jerry B 'Devil' Houston and RIO Lt Kevin T Moore), entered the fray to protect the Vigilante.

It is worth noting that the Navy came close to scoring two kills that day, for the F-4s flown by Teague and Houston engaged four MiG-17s, and Teague managed to launch a Sidewinder against one of the communist jets. The AIM-9 exploded close enough to damage the MiG, but in the ensuing battle Teague lost track of it and a kill could not be confirmed. Teague and Howell launched a second Sidewinder against another MiG, but it had been launched too close to arm and failed to detonate. The section eventually evaded the remaining jets, who outnumbered the VF-51 crews, and returned safely to their carrier.

Stillinger and Weigand listened to the engagement until vectored north-west at 15,000 ft by *Red Crown*, switching to strike frequency 'Miramar Tower' on 315.6 UHF,

and assuming combat spread formation with Weigand on Stillinger's starboard wing. Their station was 50 miles north of Quan Lang, where they could intercept the MiGs fleeing to their bases. However, no sooner had the Phantom IIs arrived on station when they received another call from *Red Crown* telling them that they had 'bogies' in their area.

The initial vector positioned a 'bogey' at 326 degrees and 14 nautical miles, about 80 degrees to their right. *Red Crown* called the bogey at eight and then six nautical miles, but no radar or visual contact could be acquired. *Red Crown* then called 'Merge plot', which meant that the VF-111 jets were almost on top of the MiGs, yet neither crew saw them. 'No Joy! No Joy!', hollered Stillinger.

Senior Chief Nowell came back with 'Look low, look low, three miles'. Lt Wiegand remembers, 'We rolled up into a left bank, looked down, and there was the MiG! It looked as though he had just pulled his nose up to come after us'. The Phantom II pilots had visually sighted a MiG-17, low, at 'ten o'clock', and at a height of approximately 500-1000 ft. 'Tally ho!' Stillinger called, followed a couple of seconds later by Weigand's, 'Roger, Tally ho on one MiG-17!' The section was in a starboard turn at about 3000 ft, descending and picking up airspeed, when the silver MiG was sighted.

Bill Freckleton later praised Senior Chief Nowell's reading of the situation on his radar scope. 'If he hadn't told us to look down exactly when he said to, we would have continued our starboard turn and the MiG would have come around behind our section and bagged one or both of us'. Such a timely intervention would mark out Senior Chief Nowell as the fighter crews' favourite controller – crews would soon call him by name during radio communications with *Red Crown*. Nowell summed up his role in one sentence. 'My job is to draw the pilot a continuous mental picture of where he is in relation to the overall tactical situation'.

Freckleton continued, 'We knew it was going to be pretty much an energy fight since the MiG could easily out-turn the F-4. We had to use our speed and energy to climb, dive, extend and pitch back, as opposed to laying on a 6G turn that would not get us inside the MiG's turn radius'.

Stillinger directed Weigand to go to trail. 'I'm engaging, go to cover', he radioed. Pitching over the top, Stillinger fell in trail on the MiG from a barrel-roll manoeuvre. As he was descending in a starboard turn, a little outside of the MiG's turn radius, the VPAF jet suddenly reversed left and pulled up hard into him. After the engagement, Stillinger later recalled, 'I don't know if he saw us or if his GCI said there was somebody behind him, but he turned'. Stillinger followed the MiG through several reversals, looking at its 'six o'clock' area, but he could not get his nose on it.

The MiG manoeuvred fairly level, with turns from 15-20 degrees nose high to 15-20 degrees nose low, while Stillinger continued to work in the vertical. Each time the F-4 pilot came off high and started his nose down toward the MiG, it would reverse its turn, positioning Stillinger on the inside. This forced Stillinger to repeatedly barrel-roll or high-speed 'yo-yo' away from the MiG to regain his position.

Stillinger continued manoeuvring until, as he related, 'I decided, "To hell with maintaining energy". I decided to pull the aeroplane around the corner and shoot him. I was outside his plane of turn, looking up at him, and I could see his tailpipe. I had a very good tone'. However, as Stillinger

Devoid of all external stores, VF-111's 'CAG bird' closes on CVA-43's steel deck during CARQUALs (carrier qualification) in the spring of 1972. CVW-15 had two CAGs for its 1971-72 *WestPac*, its original CO, Cdr Thomas E Dunlop, being killed over North Vietnam in an A-7E on 6 April 1972. He was replaced by Cdr Roger E 'Blinky' Sheets, who led CVW-15 for the remaining three months of its deployment (*via Peter E Davies*)

Although US naval vessels are 'dry', which precluded the traditional toasting of aerial success with a suitably alcoholic libation, one of the ship's galley staff could always be relied upon to rustle up a suitably decorated cake in short order! Photographed in the 'Sundowners'' ready room, the four crewmen involved in the 6 March MiG-17 kill prepare to hand out the cake to all and sundry. They are, from left to right, Lt(jg) William 'Farkle' Freckleton ('Old Nick 201's' RIO), Lt Garry 'Greyhound' Weigand (the pilot of 'Old Nick 201'), Lt James 'Yosemite' Stillinger (section leader on the 'MiG killing' mission) and Lt(jg) Rick Olin (Stillinger's RIO) (*via Brad Elward*)

pulled the trigger at a range of 4500-6000 ft, the MiG rolled into him and pulled extremely hard.

Stillinger recalls, 'That was the first time he (the MiG pilot) really turned his aeroplane to its maximum. At least that turn was much tighter than anything he showed me before'. His AIM-9 made one small twist as it tried to turn back to the target, but then went ballistic. 'I don't think it ever had a good chance', Stillinger continued, 'once the MiG pilot rolled his aeroplane and pulled extremely hard. He blanked out my view of the tailpipe, and I didn't have a tone on my next missile'.

Stillinger again tried to roll away and come back down, but the MiG-17 generated 'quite a bit of angle-off in that one turn'. Deciding that there was no way that he could get another shot better than the one he had taken, Stillinger radioed Weigand, 'I can't stay behind him. I'm going to unload and run. Do you have me in sight?' Weigand and Freckleton replied in the affirmative, having pulled above the engagement to a 'cover' position for Stillinger. Now perched to take over the fight, Weigand told his leader, 'I am rolling in on the MiG'.

Once Stillinger established that Weigand and Freckleton had the engaged MiG in sight and were positioned for an attack, he manoeuvred his Phantom II into a pure-pursuit attack. He put his nose on the MiG and lit the afterburners coming downhill. 'As I went by him' Stillinger said, 'I went ahead and relaxed the G and rolled away a little bit, almost wings-level, passed 500 ft behind him, then rolled back and pulled so I was sure I could see him. This was where his slow roll-rate was pretty obvious. I went by and he lazily rolled the aeroplane around toward me, and it made for his own lateral separation. It took him so long to roll into

a tracking position that I think he was outside gun range because I never saw him fire at me.'

Now on the defensive, Stillinger called Weigand in from overhead while he continued to extend. Keeping the MiG at his right 'four o'clock' low, Stillinger began to 'drag him out'. The MiG pilot lit his afterburner and drove towards Stillinger's 'six o'clock' in an effort to close for a missile shot, but did not enter a lead-pursuit track. According to Freckleton, Weigand kept his 'eyes padlocked' on the MiG while he swivelled his head, watching their 'six'. With the radar out, Freckleton had little to do in the back seat but post watch for bandits. Garry Weigand, on the other hand, was busy earning his flying pay.

'I rolled up over the top of the MiG, then continued around in a left-hand roll, coming out below and behind the MiG. I figured that he was preoccupied with Jim, and had not seen me. He pulled hard into Jim, who was now running straight out. Then, just as I put my nose on him, he straightened up and pulled hard into me! I figured he had now seen me, and was going to come around and start fighting with me. But I pushed down, trying to get into his "blind six", and then he reversed back onto the flight lead, who was now directly in front of him – he hadn't seen me after all!

'When I had first rolled in on him I had a lot of excess airspeed, and had started to overshoot. To correct this, I went to idle and put the speed brakes out. As the MiG pilot reversed onto the lead, he lit his 'burner and got his speed up pretty good. I got the speed brakes in and went to military. The MiG was fairly close to Jim, but his reverse had cost him some position, and Jim had picked up a lot of energy when he unloaded. We were down to 500 ft and Jim was pushing 600 knots. Jim was opening on him pretty fast. The MiG must have thought he had a chance at a gunshot though, and that's why he lit his 'burner and continued to jockey for position.'

Seconds later, Stillinger called to Weigand 'Okay, the MiG is now back at my right "four o'clock". Shoot him, shoot him. We're holding him off'. As Stillinger said, 'Shoot him', Weigand moved directly behind the MiG and fired an AIM-9D. 'Garry and I were "dead six" (to the MiG), a half-mile away at 500 knots when we shot', Freckleton remembers. The missile went directly up the MiG's tailpipe and exploded. Both F-4B crews saw several large pieces of the MiG's tail come off as it continued straight ahead for a while and then started to pitch over.

Freckleton continues. 'We entered a starboard turn to avoid the flying debris. I didn't see the impact because it was "dead 12 o'clock", but I got a good eyeful of the debris flying past on our port side. The MiG crashed into the ground and erupted in a huge fireball. The pilot was killed'.

But the crew had little time to bask in the glory of their success, for moments later *Red Crown* called 'MiGs!' Weigand again. 'By this time the North Vietnamese Air Defence Controller had vectored four MiG-21s onto us. They were only about 15 miles away, and closing fast. We were low on fuel and couldn't afford another engagement, so we lit the 'burners and exited North Vietnam, supersonic at 1200 ft, outdistancing the MiG-21s. Once in the relative safety of our own naval forces, we refuelled and returned to the *Coral Sea*'.

Garry Weigand and Bill Freckleton's kill earned them both a Silver Star, and it marked the second victory for the *Coral Sea* (VF-151 had

Weigand and Freckleton are literally mobbed on the deck of the *Coral Sea* in front of 'Old Nick 201' just minutes after shutting down and getting out of the jet on the afternoon of 6 March 1972. Note the proliferation of gear attached to the pilot's upper torso harness (*via Angelo Romano*)

claimed a MiG-17 on 6 October 1965) and the second for their Phantom II, BuNo 153019. On 20 December 1966, while flying with VF-213, it had downed a VPAF An-2.

INVASION

On 30 March 1972, the long predicted North Vietnamese invasion of South Vietnam commenced. Thirteen of the North Vietnamese Army's fourteen divisions were involved in a three-pronged assault dubbed the 'Easter Offensive' or 'Spring Invasion'. NVA troops and armour stormed across the DMZ into the Central Highlands, and across the Cambodian border towards Saigon.

Immediately, President Richard Nixon ordered strikes against the invaders, and urgently despatched more aircraft to the region. Only two carriers were on *Yankee Station* at the time, but soon there would be six, establishing a record for the entire war.

Operation *Freedom Train* began on 5 April, as more air power poured into the region. These strikes were the first large-scale attacks to be flown above the 20th Parallel since 1968, and Navy aeroplanes completed a total of 680 sorties during the first week of April. This marked a significant change from the *Rolling Thunder* campaign, where many lucrative targets were declared off limits by American politicians.

During April, Task Force 77 had swelled in size to include five carriers – *Constellation* (CVA-64), *Kitty Hawk* (CVA-63), *Hancock* (CVA-19), *Coral Sea* (CVA-43) and *Saratoga* (CV-60). And this massing of American air power would lead to the first Navy air-to-air loss of 1972 on 27 April (see *Osprey Combat Aircraft 29 - MiG-21 Units of the Vietnam War* for a full description of the action). F-4B BuNo 153025 of VF-51's Lt Al Molinare and RIO Lt Cdr J B Souder was brought down by an R-3S (K-13 Atoll) missile fired by Hoang Quoc Dung, who was flying a silver MiG-21PFM of the 921st 'Sao Do' Fighter Regiment.

REVENGE FOR VF-51

On 6 May a section of two F-4Bs from VF-51 were assigned as TARCAP for a 19-aeroplane Alpha strike on the airfield at Bai Thuong, situated 25 miles west of Thanh Hoa. Lead (F-4B BuNo 150456, call sign 'Screaming Eagle 100') was flown by Lt Cdr Jerry 'Devil' Houston and his RIO Lt Kevin Moore, with Chuck Schroeder and Rick Webb as their wing.

Expectations were high of meeting MiGs, for intelligence from the evening prior had indicated that there were 14 enemy aircraft at Bai Thuong, and that the runway was in good shape. The plan of attack called for the strike force to approach the target from the south and split into two groups, with the TARCAP coming in with the higher, slower bombers (A-6As with Rockeye munitions) in the second group.

Once through the throng of well-wishers, Weigand and Freckleton descended one level below the flight deck to VF-111's ready room, where this photograph was taken. RIO Freckleton remembers, 'We had been surrounded by an entire flightdeck of men who swarmed up to congratulate us. We made our way to the VF-111 ready room, where the ship's photographer told us he wanted one more shot. He said "Smile, and give the victory sign". One of us complied. The other was giving the peace sign!' (*William C Freckleton via Peter E Davies*)

On 6 May 1972 it was the turn of VF-111's sister-squadron VF-51 to celebrate an aerial kill, when squadron Operations Officer Lt Cdr Jerry 'Devil' Houston (second from left) and Lt Kevin Moore (extreme left) 'bagged' a MiG-17 near Bai Thuong airfield. Flying wing for the crew were Lt Cdr Chuck Schroeder (second from right) and Lt Rick Webb (extreme right). Schroeder was VF-51's Maintenance Officer, and he was in charge of keeping the unit's F-4s airworthy, as Jerry Houston explains;

'It was exciting news when VF-51 found out it was receiving F-4Bs in place of its F-8s. What we didn't know was that our F-4s would be coming from USMC rejects. The jets we were assigned had been preserved in whatever state they had been in a couple of years earlier when the Corps had declared them unairworthy. Maintenance *Tiger Teams* from all the F-4 squadrons at Miramar were assigned the job of going to MCAS El Toro and performing overdue scheduled maintenance, and getting those hulks capable of flying to Miramar. Chuck Schroeder succeeded in the Herculean undertaking of getting those over-the-hill rustbuckets ready for deployment, despite competing against my back-breaking training schedule.'

Here, RIO Webb is describing how *he* would have fought the MiGs that they had encountered earlier in the day, much to the amusement of his squadronmates (*Jerry Houston*)

As the strike force went 'feet-dry', *Red Crown* called '"Screaming Eagles", heads up' – a pre-arranged signal meaning that the MiGs had gone to strip alert, and that airborne activity was imminent. Almost immediately, the first group of A-6As began giving numerous calls of MiGs in the area. According to the Intruder crews, some of the MiGs were doing 'touch-and-goes' on the Bai Thuong runway, while others circled overhead. The latter jets scattered when the strike aircraft appeared, indicating that the MiGs were possibly being flown by rookie pilots.

As the F-4s continued inbound with the second wave of A-6As, the fighter crews monitored UHF strike transmissions. Apparently, a dark-camouflaged MiG-17 was attacking three Intruders from the first group who were egressing in front of Houston's flight. Moore quickly spotted the Intruders and the communist jet, calling 'Tally Ho. There's your A-6s . . . one . . . two . . . three . . . and here's your MiG!' Houston peered out of the cockpit until he could see them too. 'I looked out to my "two o'clock" and spotted the MiG. He was painted black, grey and white in a normal terrain-type camouflage. It was a MiG-17, and it was very easy to recognise, although I wasn't close enough to spot any national markings'.

Houston manoeuvred for position using a 6G, descending 180-degree starboard turn, jettisoning his centreline tank in the process. 'It was a clean pickle', he remembers, 'except for one bent Sparrow that we found out about later. I felt comfortable "pickling" it (the centreline tank) under any speed conditions with G on the aircraft, and was not concerned with it coming back and hitting the aeroplane'.

Schroeder had been holding a combat-spread formation on Houston's left side at the time the flight began the right descending turn. During the manoeuvre, the trailing Phantom II was forced to cross over, and ended up about 3000 ft away at Houston's 'five o'clock' at roll-out. He at once came under attack from a second MiG-17. Moore saw the second MiG about 3000 ft behind Schroeder and called twice for him to break, but without response. 'Kevin called the MiG, but in our particular aeroplane, which was old and had a history of radio problems, the Sidewinder tone was also transmitted, effectively blocking the rest of the transmission', Houston explained.

With the MiG now closing, Moore made two more 'break' calls, but there was still no acknowledgement. As Schroeder later recalled, 'I didn't hear anything. The Sidewinder tone was on, and every time we pulled G the radio would go to about half strength'. Houston again. 'Chuck didn't know about the MiG behind him until the bright red 37 mm "golf balls" began whistling by his canopy!' He immediately began a left defensive turn, with the MiG following.

Houston had been oblivious to all this, for he was busy chasing his camouflaged MiG. 'I had the blinders on, concentrating on our MiG'. Directly in front of the enemy jet was a solitary A-6A, shooting across North Vietnam at 450-475 knots at an altitude of just 100 ft. Houston quickly moved behind the MiG-17, closing at nearly 600 knots and placing himself within Sidewinder missile range. He had a solid lock-on tone.

Unknown to Houston or Moore, the A-6A that was now coming under fire from the VPAF jet was being flown by CVW-15's CAG (Commander Air Group), Cdr Roger 'Blinky' Sheets, a former fighter pilot. Flying an S-turn, Sheets had managed to position his Intruder between the MiG and the two other VMA(AW)-224 A-6As that the VF-51 crew had spotted when they first arrived on the scene. This selfless manoeuvre had seen the CAG drag the MiG onto his jet, and away from his flightmates.

With the A-6 travelling at such a high subsonic speed, Houston and Moore knew that the MiG-17 was flying too fast for its flight controls to function properly. 'At that particular speed the MiG-17 pilot had a problem. He didn't have control authority to do very much, since he lacked the power-assist on his controls. In fact, the controls got so stiff that it was actually possible to bend the stick without getting control response', recounts 'Devil' Houston.

Apparently Sheets knew this too, which was why he continued to lead the MiG. He hoped that the F-4 crew would trigger a missile, at which time the CAG would break away, knowing that the MiG could not break with him.

While Houston was now in a prime position for a missile launch on the MiG, he also ran the risk of hitting the A-6A. He called repeatedly for the Intruders to 'break right' to enable him to shoot, but only two of them appeared to follow his break call. Houston describes his thoughts at this moment. 'We were behind the MiG for a long time with good tone and we couldn't, or wouldn't, shoot because he was directly behind the A-6. Although we had our pipper on the MiG and were getting good tone, we couldn't be sure that the tone wasn't being produced by the A-6 as well, and we couldn't get the bomber pilot to break. Here was the opportunity we had waited all our lives for and it was going to worms because the A-6 wouldn't break!'

Houston wondered if it was his radio which was giving him trouble, preventing his 'Break' calls from

Another kill, another cake. All four crewmen from VF-51 are joined in their ready room by other participants in the 6 May mission, namely Marine Corps Capt Charlie Carr (CAG's Bombardier/Navigator on 6 May, and assigned to VMA(AW)-224 – front row, extreme left), CAG Cdr Roger 'Blinky' Sheets (described by 'Devil' Houston as a 'Don Knotts look-a-like, with more guts than a slaughterhouse' – front row, second from left) and Capt Bill Harris, captain of the *Coral Sea* (back row, right) (*Jerry Houston*)

being received by the A-6 crew. His F-4B was an ex-Marine Corps jet that had had its UHF radio modified to carry the AIM-9 tone when in use. 'The Marines had modified their radios to transmit the Sidewinder growl over the UHF radio when the transmit button was pressed. The transmitted tone overrode all other UHF transmissions, and effectively put us without communications during the most important couple of minutes in my airborne career. I didn't know that Sheets couldn't hear my frantic calls to "Break and get the hell out of there". All he heard was the transmitted Sidewinder tone', remembers Houston.

Having reached minimum Sidewinder launch range, Houston squeezed the trigger from 'dead six o'clock', about 3000 ft behind the MiG. 'The AIM-9G came off and went straight down, then straight up! And as we flew through the hump-backed smoke trail of the Sidewinder, it straightened out and headed for the MiG. CAG Sheets saw the missile come off the rail and broke, having played the role of ultimate decoy to the end! The MiG couldn't break, and the Sidewinder flew up his tailpipe, blowing his tail off. We were so low that the explosion of the missile was followed immediately – just bam! bam! – by the explosion the MiG made as it impacted the karst ridge'.

From after action reports, it appears that the MiG pilot had given such complete attention to shooting down the A-6A that he was never aware of Houston's presence.

MORE MiG KILLS

But the day had not ended for the American carrier aircrews. The attack against Bai Thuong airfield by CVW-15 had been a major success, and the call immediately went out for a follow-up strike. *Coral Sea's* bombers had cratered the runway, and it appeared that the MiG-17s were trapped on the ground. *Kitty Hawk's* CVW-11 responded by cancelling cyclic ops and immediately readying a number of aircraft for an Alpha strike. The rush to launch the strike caused some problems, with a number of jets being sent aloft without first being properly reconfigured, while others, such as the VF-114 'Aardvarks' jet of Lt Cdr Pete 'Viper' Pettigrew (F-4J BuNo 157245, call sign 'Linfield 201') received less than a full complement of missiles – instead of the traditional four Sparrows and four

Houston and Moore were flying VF-51's CAG jet when they claimed their MiG, this aircraft boasting a multi-coloured rendition of the unit's famous 'Screaming Eagle' motif. Dubbed the 'supersonic can opener' by rival fighter crews, this scheme was possibly the most flamboyant worn by any F-4 unit. Jerry Houston remembers;

'This scheme came about following a competition within VF-51 to design a squadron paint scheme. The Miramar wags said all the design lacked were mud flaps and a long racoon tail on some aerial!'

This photograph was taken prior to the unit deploying in November 1971 (*via Peter E Davies*)

Capt Harris congratulates Houston and Moore on the flightdeck on 6 May 1972. 'Devil' claims that he 'kept his sunglasses on to hide tears of joy' (*Jerry Houston*)

VF-114 also got in on the 'MiG killing' act on 6 May 1972 when a pair of MiG-21s were destroyed by this quartet of 'Aardvarks', (from left to right), Lt Bob Hughes, Lt(jg) Joe Cruz, Lt(jg) Mike McCabe and Lt Cdr Pete 'Viper' Pettigrew (*via Angelo Romano*)

Sidewinders, Pettigrew's aircraft received just two of each.

Two F-4Js from VF-114 were hastily scheduled to launch as one of two fighter sections assigned to separate stations to cover the evening Alpha strike against Bai Thuong. The western section, designated for MiGCAP, was on station north of Bai Thuong, while the eastern section, designated for BARCAP, was stationed 'feet-wet' off the coast of Thanh Hoa. At the start of the operation, Lt Robert G Hughes and RIO Lt(jg) Adolph J Cruz were flying MiGCAP (in F-4J BuNo 157249, call sign 'Linfield 206') with the squadron XO, Cdr John Pitson, while Lt Cdr Pete Pettigrew and RIO Lt(jg) Michael J McCabe were part of the BARCAP.

When Pitson experienced a radar failure during rendezvous, he switched with Pettigrew and McCabe, and they assumed lead of the western station. TARCAP for the strike was provided by the 'Aardvark's' sister squadron, VF-213 'Black Lions'.

Crossing the beach over the 'hourglass' rivers north-east of Thanh Hoa, Pettigrew and Hughes were flying at about 10,000 ft and 420 knots on the way to their station when they received a vector from *Red Crown*, aboard the *Chicago*. The section remained in military power and descended to about 8000 ft in combat-spread formation, heading 250 degrees. At about ten nautical miles 'feet dry', they picked up a strobe (contact) on their RHAW (Radar Homing And Warning) system emanating from behind them.

Lt Cdr Pettigrew later recalled, 'The whole squadron had been briefed that in order to protect our "six", we would cross-turn, which is not a very good offensive manoeuvre, but is an exceptionally good defensive one. We made one cross-turn because of the AI (air intercept) strobe, then returned to our original course and picked up the same AI strobe. We were heading back in the direction of "feet-wet" by this time, and realised that the strobe was triggered from the ground, so we cross-turned again and went back on our original vector.'

But this manoeuvring did not end their problems. *Red Crown* then called a 'bogey', and directed them south, only for the Phantom IIs to intercept elements of their own strike package. Vectoring back onto their original course, the crew were relieved to hear the voice of a new controller on the radio – Senior Chief Larry Nowell, the famed *Red Crown* 'ace' aboard the *Chicago*.

The Phantom II crews continued down towards Bai Thuong, where they picked up the TARCAP which was apparently the target of their original vector. About this time *Red Crown* came up and said, 'I have a new contact. Come starboard 010 degrees. Contact is 010 for 30 miles'.

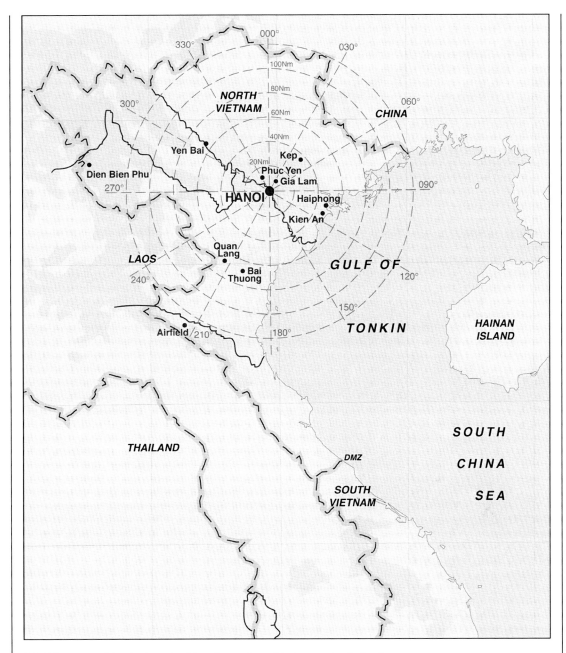

McCabe was working in the pulse-Doppler mode at this time, and called, 'Contact 330 at 25'. He locked-up the return and called a 900-knot closing velocity before the radar broke lock when the MiG went to beam.

At about 15 nautical miles Lt Hughes reacquired the contact and secured another radar lock-up. Pettigrew immediately called his wingman. 'I'll go shooter. You've got the VID (visual identification)', then slid back slightly off the port side of 'Linfield 206', with a separation distance of about one nautical mile.

The section went into minimum afterburner at 12 nautical miles and continued to close on the bandits. McCabe made first contact, and described the situation;

Red Crown fighter controllers used a *Bullseye* brevity code during the *Linebacker I* and *II* operations to provide guidance for aircrews – *Bullseye* represented Hanoi. A MiG sighting near Kep, for example, would be conveyed as, '*Bullseye*, 45 for 40', meaning that the MiG was at 060 degrees from Hanoi, and 40 nautical miles out

'We were proceeding along the ridge about 30-35 miles north of Thanh Hoa (210 degrees at 40 nautical miles from *Bullseye* – the codename for Hanoi, which was used as a reference point for broadcast reports on the position of NVAF fighters) when I picked the MiGs up at "ten o'clock" about four miles away, 4000 ft low. We were at 7000 ft, about 3000 feet above the karst. The first section was at about "10-11 o'clock". There were four MiGs in a kind of "box-four" formation, and the wingmen were flying a tactical wing position known as "welded wing". MiGs' one and two were so close that they generated a single "paint" on the radar. My aircraft commander called a turn into them for positive identification, and from that point on we were in the engagement.'

As the MiGs approached, passing underneath the Phantom IIs, they emerged from out of the sun. It appeared that they had still not seen the F-4s. 'Through most of it', McCabe continues, 'I kept track of the first section, which eventually made it all the way around to our "one o'clock", just one mile away, but they never did get into any kind of firing position. Their noses were always 70-90 degrees off'.

Pettigrew added, 'We had visually acquired all four enemy jets, and from the time we first spotted them, we never lost sight of any of them throughout the engagement. It was now about 1830 hrs, and we were low, looking into the sun to see them. When the sun goes down and you're looking into a haze, sometimes an aeroplane will show up very well at long range because it's much darker than any of the surrounding haze. This is how they appeared – very, very dark shaped aeroplanes, which stood out very well'.

Pettigrew and Hughes then turned into the jets of the second section, which were performing a shallow left turn. According to Pettigrew, who described the initial attack, 'They didn't have much airspeed, so we immediately had about 90 degrees off on them. You might almost call it a hat stern conversion – quite a bit hotter than you would want to run. However, they didn't seem to be turning very hard. In fact, the first section continued back to almost our "7-8 o'clock" before they really started turning, which gave them so much distance behind us that they never got back into the fight again. Since Hughes was outside of my turn, which put him in a better position as a shooter, I said, "You're engaged, I'm free – go get him".'

Hughes pressed the attack, picking the fourth MiG, which was in the outside rear position flying as wing for the section leader. Rolling in from a high angle-off (which he estimated as 'about 45 degrees'), Hughes

Handed over to the Navy at St Louis on 24 September 1969, BuNo 157245, was issued new to VF-114 on 24 September 1969. The fighter would serve with the unit for no less than six years, and by the time it left the 'Aardvarks' in December 1975, the jet had completed four *WestPacs* (two of which were combat tours) and downed a MiG-21 on 6 May 1972. When VF-114 commenced it conversion onto the F-14 in January 1976, BuNo 157245 was transferred to VF-51. Its time with the 'Screaming Eagles' lasted just a matter of months, for in May it was sent to NARF North Island for heavy maintenance. The fighter returned to service exactly one year later, when it was flown to Kaneohe Bay to join VMFA-212. Transferred to fellow-Kaneohe residents VMFA-232 on 13 October 1977, the jet remained with this unit until September 1979. BuNo 157245 then returned to Miramar to serve with VF-121, and it stayed at 'Fightertown USA' until flown to nearby NARF North Island on 30 September 1980 to commence its upgrade to F-4S specification. Emerging from rework in June of the following year, the Phantom II was issued to VF-103, and it served with the Oceana-based unit until December 1982. BuNo 157245 participated in the unit's solitary Mediterranean cruise with the F-4S aboard *Forrestal* in 1982. Transferred to VMFA-251 at Beaufort, the jet served with the Marines until 29 August 1985, when it was flown to Davis-Monthan AFB for storage. It had completed 4582 flight hours by the time of its arrival. Stricken from the Navy's inventory on 9 August 1995, this aircraft is still resident within AMARC today (*via Angelo Romano*)

thought that the trailing MiG was 'kind of outside the envelope, but I had this good tone'. Hughes report of the action continues;

'I said, "Jesus, MiG-21, good tone – maybe I'll never see this again", so I pulled the trigger. The Sidewinder came off and went out to the right, underneath my nose. I thought I'd wasted a round, but about that time you could tell it was pulling itself back in, and it ripped off part of the MiG's tail. It didn't appear to me that he ever saw me, or knew that I was coming.'

When Hughes fired, he was about 45 degree angle-off, flying at 480 knots some 3000 ft above the ground. The MiG was just 1.6 nautical miles away.

After downing his target, Hughes was only a few degrees off position for a successful attack on the next MiG. Closing rapidly, he slid his throttles into idle to prevent further closure inside the 6000-ft range he now had. 'The MiG started to pull harder', Hughes said. 'I was looking right up his tailpipe from a distance of about a mile. I got a tone and pulled the trigger. However, by the time the Sidewinder came off the rail after pulling the trigger I'd lost the tone. I tried it again, got another tone, pulled it again, and the same thing happened once more! I was really pissed by this time. I had wasted two good 'Winders, and I didn't know if it was my fault or if the guy was really "warping my cone"'.

Both rounds missed. 'The first went off to the right', Hughes explained, 'and the other went ballistic to the inside of the turn'. Apparently the MiG was not in afterburner for either of the missile shots.

Obtaining yet another good tone, Hughes squeezed off his last AIM-9 and watched as it shredded off pieces of the MiG's tail when it detonated.

Having literally just stepped out of his jet and onto the flightdeck of CVA-63, Lt Bob Hughes is warmly greeted by the carrier's CO. Having survived his combat tour, Bob Hughes would later perish on 31 January 1979 in a mid-air collision between a TA-4J (BuNo 154288) of VF-126 and an F-4J (BuNo 153878) of VF-121. Serving as an adversary pilot with VF-126, Hughes was leading two Skyhawks in a two-v-two free-flight manoeuvring evolution at 25,000 ft off the California coast, near San Diego. The lead Phantom II was being chased in a turn by Hughes in his TA-4J at 25,000 ft when the pilot of F-4J BuNo 153858 attempted to come to the aid of his leader by allegedly performing an out-of-order 'blind lead turn' into his adversary – a manoeuvre that was strictly prohibited during ACM training. The end result of this turn was that the VF-121 jet collided with the pursuing Skyhawk, rendering the F-4J uncontrollable and forcing the crew to eject. Both men were quickly recovered with minor injuries. Neither the TA-4J or its two crewmen (Hughes's passenger was VF-121 RIO Tom Rippinger, who was catching a bonus hop) were found, however, despite a detailed search of the surrounding waters (*via Peter Mersky*)

At almost the same time he saw another missile go directly up the MiG-21's tailpipe, blowing the aircraft to pieces.

Pettigrew, meanwhile, had seen Hughes' down the first MiG, and then saw him go for its leader. He recalls telling his RIO, 'That SOB isn't going to get the next one too', and then pulling into hard 8G turn just as the communist pilot broke to the inside of Hughes's F-4. As Pettigrew broke and headed for the MiG, Hughes fired his second and third missiles. Continuing its hard turn, the MiG-21 was rapidly dissipating energy, while both Phantom IIs were closing at about 480 knots. Pettigrew again;

'I got back on the inside of the turn a little bit aft of Hughes at a height of 800 ft. We were both within ten degrees of the MiG's tail, and I looked up and pulled my nose up onto the MiG. By this time, he was at a height of about 4000 ft, and I got a tone and went to "arm". I was pulling to the inside of the turn, and just as I was about to fire, I saw another missile come off Hughes's aeroplane. I think I fired about the same time that his missile came off the rail. We had about a one-second difference in the missiles.

'We were really close inside by now. I figured I was down to about 2500 ft, with about ten degrees off, when I fired. I pitched the nose up and rolled right because I was overshooting badly. Continuing to roll right, I pulled back on the stick a little bit and saw the missile go all the way up the MiG's tailpipe, before reversing roll to the left.

'Hughes's missile hit first, knocking pieces off the stabilator, and about a second later mine hit and the aeroplane disintegrated. There wasn't anything left of it. I pulled the nose of my jet up higher because I was starting to run into the debris of the MiG, and as I flew some 200 ft wide of the point of impact, the pilot's 'chute opened just off my left wing – we almost ran into him.'

The entire engagement had lasted for little more than a minute. It was simply a 360-degree turning fight, which had taken place in the horizontal plane. Both VF-114 crews had the advantage throughout the engagement, and the MiGs made no attempt to turn in the vertical.

The lead section of MiG-21s, meanwhile, had now turned around and were two miles in-trail, but they were unable to close. *Red Crown* advised

Mission almost over, an F-4J from VF-114 powers its way towards a three-wire trap aboard *Kitty Hawk* during May 1972. One of the Navy's most successful fighter units in terms of aerial victories, VF-114 was credited with two MiG-17s, two MiG-21s and an An-2 destroyed during the Vietnam conflict. Its highest scoring pilot was Lt 'Denny' Wisely, who claimed a MiG-17 and the solitary An-2 during his tour with the 'Aardvarks' in 1966-67. At that stage in the war, the unit's F-4Bs were a little more subtly marked, lacking the diagonal fuselage stripe. Not overly impressed with the latter adornment, Wisely told the Editor that 'the big orange stripe made the aircraft look like a Coast Guard cutter'! (*via Peter Mersky*)

Pettigrew and Hughes about them, calling 'Four miles behind you. They are no threat, get the hell out 120 degrees'. Both F-4 pilots unloaded down into the karst and adopt a tight spread-formation. They also continued to jink until the SAM threat had passed. When the Phantom IIs were about halfway out, *Red Crown* finally called and said, 'Okay, they've turned away – no threat'.

After rendezvousing with their tanker, Pettigrew and Hughes returned to the carrier. The former describes their return as follows;

'We came back to the ship and asked them for a low pass. There was a big thunder storm right off the bow of the ship on the left hand side. We came on down, and of course neither of us could fly worth a damn by this time because we were shaking so much. We came in for a victory pass with the hooks down, "fogged over", looking up at the ship, and there is an A-6 with his gear down on the right hand side, a helo coming right across, and a guy rolling into the groove, all above us! So we closed our eyes, went through that, picked our noses up, and went into our victory roll and right into a thunder storm. That was the worst part of the whole engagement, trying to do the victory pass!'

In reviewing the incident, Pete Pettigrew later commented, 'We were talking the whole time. It's not very difficult after you've done it so many times before. I thought I'd seen this type of fight fought before against A-4s. A lot of things become instinctive. Hughes and I had never flown together before, yet we had no problem at all communicating. I think we knew exactly what each of us was thinking, or all four people knew exactly what the others were thinking the whole time. I think it's primarily because of the training'.

Mike McCabe added, 'All the way through this engagement my helmet was slid down over my eyes. When I turned around and we pulled 8G, my mask came right off my face and they (the MiGs) were at "seven o'clock". I had to take both my hands and put the mask up to talk!'

Bob Hughes remembered, 'There was no question about the fact that Pettigrew was on my wing the whole time. He crossed a couple of times to keep inside of the turn or abeam of me, and called out his position, so I knew exactly where he was the whole time we were going in. That was really nice knowing you have the support to go ahead and attack with somebody there to watch out for you'.

According to the *Red Baron* authors, both Pettigrew and Hughes 'demonstrated a high degree of mutual support and co-ordination during this engagement. They were able to take advantage of the element of surprise, achieve two quick kills, and separate from the area without being seriously threatened by any of the MiGs. Good radio procedures enabled them to effectively press home their attack'.

DOUBLE KILL

VPAF jets were next encountered just 48 hours after VF-114's successful engagement on 6 May, and the resulting action led to the Navy being able to boast its first double-MiG killing crew of the war.

On the 8th, VF-96 was tasked with providing part of the MiGCAP support for 'Fresh Bath Alpha' – a major multi-carrier Alpha strike against a large truck-park area near Son Tay, some 25 nautical miles west of Hanoi. This mission was to be a combined Navy/Air Force effort. The

A pair of F-4Js from VF-96 drop their 500-lb Mk 82s through broken cloud at medium altitude 'somewhere over North Vietnam' in the spring of 1972. Such missions enjoyed little target accuracy unless the 'blind' Phantom IIs were being led by a ground radar-equipped A-6 Intruder. Behind 'Showtime 111' is 'Showtime 112', alias 'Randy' Cunningham and 'Willie' Driscoll's 'MiG killing' BuNo 157267 (*via Peter Mersky*)

target area contained an estimated 400 trucks, being used for both freight staging and driver training. The total attacking force consisted of 50 strike aircraft, plus large supporting forces.

Being a joint Navy/Air Force operation, several MiGCAPs were airborne. The Navy was providing CAP for its own forces, while the Air Force undertook MiGCAP coverage around the airfield at Yen Bai and north of Hanoi. 19 January 'MiG-killers' Lt Randy Cunningham and Lt (jg) Willie Driscoll crewed one of two CAP F-4Js put up by VF-96 – their jet was, in fact, 'Showtime 112', which they had employed so effectively to claim their first kill almost four months earlier.

Heading for the target, Cunningham and his usual wingman, Lt Brian 'Bulldog' Grant (along with RIO Lt Jerry Sullivan), positioned themselves about ten minutes ahead of their strike force to help clear the skies of MiGs. They entered North Vietnam as a section at the mouth of the Red River Valley Delta, 160 degrees and 75 nautical miles from Hanoi. As they went 'feet-dry', two SAMs were launched at them from north of the 'hourglass' rivers, but both missiles failed to guide and appeared to have been merely fired in their direction. More SA-2s were then launched, and 85 mm AAA also began to appear at their height, forcing Cunningham to lead his wingman down behind a nearby karst ridge in search of cover.

Proceeding towards the target area, he and Grant received a message from *Red Crown* informing them of bandits some 50 nautical miles away. However, the fighter controller quickly called again and told the section to 'skip it'. Apparently they had dropped below the hills and had broken radar contact. By now the two F-4s were 20 miles up the Red River from their assigned station, and the crews were getting nervous with the 'hide-and-seek' tactics of the MiGs. At this point they turned around and headed back south.

As they returned to their CAP station, Cunningham and Grant received another *Red Crown* vector onto four 'unknown' bandits at 340 degrees, some 20 nautical miles from their position – the direction of Yen Bai, which was then under attack by Air Force fighter-bombers. The VF-96 crews were following this vector towards the bandits when Cunningham realised that he was no longer receiving *Red Crown*. Suddenly, Grant hollered, '"Duke", in place port. Go!' Remembering a similar situation from a few weeks back where, VF-51's Al Molinare and J B Souder had been surprised by a MiG from behind in this very area, he instantly complied and banked sharply left, before engaging afterburner and pitching up into the vertical.

The section was now flying at about 450 knots at an altitude of 4000 ft (about 2000 ft above the cloud layer), with Cunningham pulling to the inside of the turn in an attempt to restore the section's com-

'Randy' Cunningham and 'Willie' Driscoll enjoy a brew (or perhaps something stronger, courtesy of the ship's doctor!) in the VF-96 ready room after downing their second MiG on the morning of 8 May 1972 (*via Angelo Romano*)

bat-spread position. As he passed through Grant's 'six', he called that his tail was clear. About ten seconds later, however, Cunningham noticed a MiG-17 coming up through the cloud layer in afterburner.

The jet closed rapidly on Grant, who did not see the threat, and began firing his 37 mm cannon at a range of about 2000 ft. 'He had popped up through the clouds and was right behind Brian and shooting!', Cunningham remembers. 'He must have been last in his class in gunnery, however, because I wasn't pulling that many Gs, yet the MiG's tracers were falling short. I called Brian and said, "You've got a MiG-17 on your tail and he's shooting! Get rid of your centreline tank, unload and outrun him'.

The two F-4 pilots immediately jettisoned their centreline tanks and Grant rolled and pulled slightly out of the path of the MiG's rounds. The communist pilot reversed and tried to get back onto Grant's tail, but the latter also reversed slightly, unloaded and kept opening the gap.

'I was really impressed', Cunningham recalled, 'by the slow roll rate that the MiG-17 has. It looks like a butterfly because it goes so slow. The MiG was probably doing between 350 and 400 knots, and it must take a gorilla in there to turn the aeroplane, because Grant would roll and the MiG would roll, super slow. Rather than have him reverse, come back, and look, I told Grant to roll and not reverse, just unload. You could see the MiG roll and pull, but he still would never pull lead. His nose was almost directly on Grant and the "BBs" (cannon rounds) were falling short. Two rolls and Grant was able to push out quite a bit beyond the MiG'.

Because Grant did not have to pull a lot of G, Cunningham was able to position his F-4 on the MiG, and he reduced his angle-off to about 40 degrees. However, as Grant completed his second roll, the VPAF fighter launched an Atoll, which took both crews by surprise. 'They briefed us that the MiG-17s didn't have Atolls', explained Cunningham, 'so it scared the hell out of me'. He screamed, 'Atoll! Break port!' He continued, 'I called another break turn. The missile guided and it started coming around the corner, but then it went to the outside and went ballistic. Right then I shot a missile that was on the edge of the envelope. It was about 35 degrees off, and I knew that the MiG could see me, but I thought he was going to shoot another Atoll, and I wanted to give him something to think about, even if it didn't hit him'.

27

As soon as Cunningham fired his first missile, the MiG broke into it. While the AIM-9 detonated immediately under its target, it apparently did no damage, leaving the MiG to renew his attack on Grant. Just as the Sidewinder had left 'Showtime 112', Cunningham heard Driscoll say, '"Duke"! Look up!' The pilot saw two MiG-17s pass directly over his canopy, about 200 ft above him, one on each side. 'I told Willie to keep an eye on them, for I figured that we had lots of time to get a shot at the first MiG before these two got turned around. I was about to get my first lesson in the turning ability of the MiG-17! They actually turned inside of each other and started down after us!' Cunningham later recounted.

As this action unfolded, one of the MiGs fired an Atoll, which passed behind 'Showtime 112' but did not detonate. Cunningham continued to press his attack as Grant disengaged from the first MiG. Reducing the angle-off to about 20 degrees from the tail of the communist jet, Cunningham squeezed off another missile.

'It looked like he (the MiG) was trying to roll the opposite way', Cunningham recalled. 'I squeezed the trigger as he rolled and the missile hit him, but it only knocked a little piece off his tail. I almost started to squeeze the trigger again when I saw a flame shoot out. He was already in 'burner, but a big flame shot out and he went into a shallow turn and crashed right into the side of a peak. There was very little structural damage to the aeroplane, but he never tried to eject'.

When Cunningham fired, Grant was about 1.5 nautical miles ahead of him, and he had two MiGs about 3000 ft behind him, blazing away with their guns. Cunningham called to Grant to 'pitch up and go vertical' to a high-perch position in order to drag the MiGs to the inside of Grant's turn so that Cunningham could get them off of his tail. But the

Rearmed and refuelled, seven Phantom IIs from VF-92 and VF-96 prepare to launch from the *Constellation* on 9 May 1972. The following day, all of these aircraft were heavily involved in the largest aerial battle of the Vietnam War. Nearest to the camera is F-4J BuNo 155769, which was used by Lts Michael Connelly and Thomas Blonski to down two MiG-17s. Alongside it is 'Silver Kite 207' (BuNo 155560), which was damaged beyond repair when struck by 85 mm flak shells. It was coaxed back to the 'Connie' on one engine by pilot Rod Dilworth. 'Showtime 110' was crewed by Lts Brian Grant and Jerry Sullivan, who occupied the wing position for 'Randy' Cunningham and 'Willie' Driscoll as the latter pair set about downing three MiGs. 'Silver Kite 212' (BuNo 155797) was shot down by the same 85 mm flak that gravely damaged 'Silver Kite 207'. Its pilot, squadron XO Cdr Harry Blackburn, was killed either during or soon after capture, and his RIO, Lt Steve Rudloff, made a PoW. Chained down to the right of 'Silver Kite 212' is 'Showtime 112' (BuNo 157267), which had of course been used by Cunningham and Driscoll to claim MiG kills on 19 January and 8 May. To its right is 'Silver Kite 210' (BuNo 155813), crewed by Lts Austin Hawkins and Charles Tinker during the morning engagement that saw Lt Curt Dosé and Lt James McDevitt claim a MiG-21 in 'Silver Kite 211' (BuNo 157269). The latter jet is the final Phantom II visible in this historic photograph (*via Angelo Romano*)

MiGs were closing. Cunningham told Driscoll, 'I'm going to use the disengagement manoeuvre. I can't drag them to the inside anymore – they're getting too close'.

As he rolled left and came down, Cunningham momentarily lost sight of the MiGs. He told Driscoll to watch the MiGs. 'Okay, one's at "five" and one's at "seven", "five" and "seven", and they're closing', the RIO replied. But Cunningham could still not visually locate the MiGs, so he reversed, pulled his nose through and finally picked up a MiG just as it fired an Atoll. He broke hard into the missile and it shot past his 'six o'clock'.

Cunningham and Driscoll now had two MiGs closing on them, one to their left and one to their right, and tracers were passing over their canopy. They were trapped. If they rolled right, the MiG on their right fired, and if they rolled left, the other MiG shot at them.

'Never break into a MiG-17', Cunningham remembered. 'I couldn't disengage. I used every ounce of strength I had and kicked the rudder (essentially performing a "snap-roll") and got the nose down almost into a defensive spiral or a high-G, nose-low barrel roll. I pulled and pegged the G-meter. I pulled panels off the top of the aeroplane, off the top of the wing and from the underside. The jet was declared down by the maintenance department when I got back to the carrier because both flaps were broken. I pulled 12G on the aeroplane. You know what the MiG-17 pilot did? He rolled to the inside and rendezvoused on me! I had nothing left, so I radioed Brian. "Two, get in here. I'm in deep trouble". I was scared'.

The MiG-17 was still on the inside of Cunningham's turn, pulling lead, with his nose bristling with muzzle flashes. Just above the top of the cloud deck, Cunningham pushed over into the undercast and immediately reversed as hard as he could, unloaded, and selected afterburner. Accelerating to 500 knots, he pitched up into the sun, thinking that it would mask his afterburner from any VPAF heat-seeking missiles. Moreover, he knew the MiG-17s could not follow him at that speed.

As two MiGs came out of the clouds after Cunningham, Grant rolled in on them from his 'seven o'clock' position overhead. The communist fighters saw Grant in pursuit and immediately disengaged, heading back down into the clouds. Both Cunningham and Grant made a couple of cross-turns searching for the MiGs, then egressed the area.

The weather cleared as the crews headed towards the beach, and they noted numerous trucks in the area. Cunningham's account continued, 'I had tried many times to get a Sidewinder tone on a truck and couldn't do it, so I flew down right along a big highway, and I don't know if the guy had bad plugs, or needed a tune-up, or what, but I got a beautiful Sidewinder tone on a big truck and shot the damned thing. I rolled in there almost supersonic, got the tone and pressed it down low, which was a dumb thing to do. It blew the devil out of the truck and really nailed it. I pitched up, rolled and took a look at my target, and the thing was flaming'.

After the engagement, Cunningham told the *Red Baron* investigators, 'It's the one thing you should get across to everybody. The MiG-17 disengagement manoeuvre, as they did it in *Have Drill*, really works. I guarantee it. In two or three unloadings, it works. Once the MiG-17s have their angle of bank established, the damned things will turn like an SOB'.

FROM *FREEDOM TRAIN TO LINEBACKER*

On 10 May 1972 Operation *Linebacker* officially commenced. Essentially an outgrowth of *Freedom Train*, the air campaign had originally, albeit briefly, been christened *Rolling Thunder*, but was soon renamed – some say to reflect President Nixon's love of football.

On this first day of *Linebacker*, the Navy refocused its attention from targets in South Vietnam, where the bulk of the ground fighting was taking place, to the coastal regions from Haiphong north to the Chinese border. In all, 173 Navy attack sorties were flown in this area on the 10th, including strikes on targets in and around the Hanoi/Haiphong area.

By this stage of the campaign, the massive US air strikes had stopped the North Vietnamese advance into South Vietnam, allowing bombing missions to be switched to disrupting and destroying the NVA's supply and logistics systems, hence the start of *Linebacker*.

10 May was clearly the most intense air-to-air combat day of the entire Vietnam War. On that day, the *Constellation* was readying three major Alpha strikes against port and storage facilities in Hon Gay, north of Haiphong. The first would be launched in the morning, with the second scheduled for midday and the third for late afternoon.

A section of two F-4Js from VF-92 (VF-96's sister-squadron on CVA-64) was providing TARCAP support for the morning Alpha force, which included four other F-4Js as flak suppressors, two A-7Es in the anti-SAM *Iron Hand* role, nine A-7Es and five A-6As as the strikers and five EKA-3B ECM/tankers. The force's targets were the Haiphong Kien An airfield and nearby AAA batteries.

Each TARCAP Phantom II was armed with four AIM-7E-2 and four AIM-9Gs apiece, with a single 600-gallon centreline tank completing the array of external stores. BuNo 157269 (call sign 'Silver Kite 211') was crewed by Topgun graduate Lt Curt 'Dozo' Dosé and RIO Lt Cdr

A spotless F-4J from VF-92 cruises over broken cloud during a training mission over the South China Sea in early 1972. This photograph was taken by future MiG killer Lt Curt Dosé. Note the crown motif stencilled onto 'Silver Kite 206's' splitter plate
(*Curt Dosé via Peter E Davies*)

Responsible for stirring up a veritable hornet's nest over Kep airfield on the morning of 10 May 1972, this quartet of 'Silver Kites' were lucky to return to the 'Connie' alive. And Lt Curt 'Dozo' Dosé (extreme right) and Lt Cdr James 'Routeslip' McDevitt (second from right) also managed to 'bag' a MiG-21 before hastily departing the area. Flying lead on this mission were Lts Austin 'Hawk' Hawkins (left) and Charles J Tinker (second from left). Hawkins had planned to probe Kep following the completion of the fighters' TARCAP support for CVW-9's Alpha strike on targets in Hon Gay. He was nearing the end of his tour, and had yet to successfully encounter any MiGs. His bold plan was unauthorised, and strictly forbidden, and he informed only his RIO, Charles Tinker, of his intentions. 'He told me there were MiGs at Kep airfield, and once our attack guys were on their way out we were going to take a look at Kep', Tinker remembers. The RIO had to promise Hawkins not to tell anyone of his plan! Tinker continues, 'Once we got back to the boat, everyone was excited about Curt's MiG kill, but "Hawk" was in deep shit for leaving the strike to go trolling. The "elephants" were still deciding our fate when we manned up for the strike on Hai Duong. We were punished by tying us to an *Iron Hand* A-7 as escort. "Hawk" was told, "If you don't come back with him, don't come back at all!"' (*via Peter Mersky*)

Lt 'Hawk' Hawkins pre-flights his F-4J, which is already secured to one of CVA-64's waist catapults (*via Angelo Romano*)

James 'Routeslip' McDevitt, with Lts Austin Hawkins and Charles J Tinker flying lead.

The initial strike was rather uneventful for the CAP crews, for although they had heard numerous MiG calls on *Guard* (emergency VHF channel monitored as a secondary frequency by all air and ground stations in the area) during ingress, neither Hawkins or Dosé could make out a visual or radar contact. However, as the strike force was leaving the area, the F-4 section again heard *Red Crown* say, 'Bandits, north-east at 35 nautical miles'. Responding to the call, the section turned into a northerly heading and made a radar search, but failed to establish contact with the reported bandits.

Looking for MiGs, Hawkins and Dosé headed toward Kep airfield, where they expected to find some enemy activity. They were flying at 6000 ft and 600 knots when they sighted the field from a distance of about eight nautical miles and manoeuvred onto a northerly heading. Dosé was in combat-spread to the left of Hawkins. Approaching the airfield, both pilots saw two MiG-19s in revetments at one end of the runway and two MiG-21s holding short at the other.

As Dosé flew over the site, he wondered how they were going to strike at the MiGs on the ground, for neither F-4 had a gun, and the Sidewinders would need more heat to track stationary targets. Suddenly, McDevitt called out, 'MiGs rolling!' He had spotted two more MiG-21s taking off!

31

Curt Dosé and Jim McDevitt pose for the camera prior to strapping into their Phantom II and manning the alert
(*Curt Dosé via Peter E Davies*)

Dosé recalled this moment. 'Sure enough, there were two MiG-21s on a section take-off, about a third of the way down the runway, accelerating towards us fast. I called for the tactical lead and said, "Come port and down". Hawkins called for afterburner, which I think I had already done, or did simultaneously, and we came slicing down in an in-place turn back along the runway at about 1000 ft. We were straddling the runway, with me on the right and Hawkins on the left.

'By this time the MiGs were airborne. They were two miles off the end of the runway when we first started coming down, and I could see they were in afterburner and were climbing pretty much straight ahead.'

As Hawkins and Dosé closed to about 1.5 nautical miles, the MiG-21s simultaneously jettisoned their centreline tanks, apparently responding to a radio call, then started pulling to port in a gentle climbing turn. The tanks hit the ground and exploded in a fireball. Both MiGs were still low – about 100 ft above the deck – when Hawkins called out, 'You take the one on the right (MiG 1), and I'll take the one on the left (MiG 2)'.

Dosé continues his account. 'I had a tone before I even looked. I did check the null while I was still closing to make sure that I had the Sidewinder on him (the MiG). There was no doubt about it. It was a beautiful tone, and we squeezed off the first Sidewinder and watched it. The missile guided very nicely, but it seemed like it took forever to come off the aeroplane, and it took forever to get there. It finally detonated immediately behind the MiG.

'I thought I had him, but he kept flying, so I immediately fired a second Sidewinder at the same MiG (MiG 1). They were in a sort of "loose-cruise", or "fighting-wing" formation at this time, not more than 100 ft apart, and they stayed that way. I fired the second Sidewinder at exactly the same track-crossing angle as the first one. I estimate that we had about 20 degrees aspect and about five degrees look-down on the MiGs.

'The second Sidewinder went down to the jet's altitude, appeared to level off, and then disappeared up its tailpipe. Nothing happened for a couple of seconds and then the whole aeroplane burst into a huge 100-ft wide ball of flame. Out of the forward edge of that ball of flame came the MiG-21, tumbling nose over tail. It did two tumbles and went into the ground with no ejection.'

When Dosé saw his second missile hit, he immediately pulled his nose into the lead MiG (MiG 2) and triggered his third Sidewinder, which guided to the MiG and detonated about ten feet behind, almost exactly as his first missile had done. Meanwhile, Hawkins had also fired two AIM-9s at the same aeroplane, and both missiles detonated just aft of and below the MiG. As Hawkins fired his third Sidewinder the MiG broke into it with a 90-degree angle of bank, giving the Phantom II pilot a perfect plan view of his target. The Sidewinder passed about 15 ft behind the MiG's tailpipe and detonated when it hit the ground.

When MiG 2 performed its breaking turn, it was doing an estimated 300 knots, and Hawkins about 550 knots. The VF-92 pilot initially pulled as hard as he could to see if there was any possibility of staying with the MiG. When it became obvious that he could not make the turn, he pulled back on the stick, shoved in rudder, and started doing high-G rolls up and around the MiG. He remarked to his RIO Tinker, 'Another 90 degrees of turn and this SOB is going to fly into the ground'. Hawkins was certain that the MiG was either going to crash or be forced to level his wings and give him another shot.

The engaged aircraft circled Kep airfield during the entire engagement, staying within about five nautical miles of the field. Dosé checked the sky above him and saw an overcast of 57 mm and 85 mm flak behind them, and also a third MiG-21 (MiG 3) at about two nautical miles, slicing down at Hawkins's 'five o'clock'. Dosé called his leader and suggested an immediate disengagement, telling him to 'Bug out', but Hawkins was now on a northerly heading, and did not want to disengage.

'No, I can get this guy', he told Dosé, and continued to press on after the second MiG-21. The third MiG closed so fast on the VF-92 jet that he passed right through Hawkins's 'six o'clock' in a lag pursuit and never presented a real threat. When Hawkins reached the southern end of the airfield, he disengaged vertically, went out, then rolled over. The second MiG pulled his nose back into Hawkins's general area and launched an Atoll. The missile, however, went ballistic and missed.

The section headed for the beach over the karst in full afterburner at just 50 ft, continuing to jink as they looked for MiG 3 in their 'six o'clock'. During their jinking manoeuvres, Hawkins and Dosé became separated, and each jet egressed alone. Hawkins exited south of Haiphong towards the 'hourglass' rivers, while Dosé exited north of the port city. They rejoined on the tanker and returned to their ship without further incident. Dosé later commented on his egress, 'If not a noble departure, it was at least a successful one at near Mach below 50 ft, with MiG-21s behind us firing Atoll missiles'.

After the flight, Austin Hawkins noted, 'The thing that I think could be learned from the engagement itself is that with the missile, look-down is the same as angle-off as far as tracking is concerned. It's something that's got to be remembered. I think something that's not stressed enough is the fact that a simple "six o'clock" shot is not good enough – you've got to know all the parameters. If you've got 200-300 knots overtake, pressing to three-quarters

Tactical Navy tankers provided a crucial lifeline to fighters during missions flown in 1972, when fuel was often used up at an alarming rate by crews that engaged afterburner for extended periods whilst chasing, or evading, MiGs, or attempting to avoid SAMs and AAA. This EKA-3B (refuelling two F-4Js from VF-92 in March 1972) was from CVW-9's VAQ-130 Det 1, and it shared the tanker duty within the wing with KA-6Ds from VA-165 and buddy tank-equipped A-7Es from VA-146 and VA-147 (*via Peter E Davies*)

of a mile or one mile, you're pushing it. The missile was guiding on the plume itself, plus the fact that it was a look-down shot as it went past the tailpipe, and the missile detonated directly below the aeroplane. I saw both of mine blow up the same way.

He also said, 'If I had it to do over again, knowing what happened to my Sidewinders, I'd make sure that I was at the same altitude as the MiGs before I'd shoot. I wouldn't shoot with any look-down. In this particular engagement a gun would have made all the difference due to the close range. It would have been no trouble at all to have achieved a

Curt Dosé uses his hands to describe to fellow VF-92 pilot Lt Cdr Gordon Williamson (back to the camera) how he manoeuvred in behind his MiG-21 before despatching it with an AIM-9G (*Aerospace Publishing*)

smooth gun-tracking position, as he was in a position where there was nothing he could do but turn. It seems that there have been so few times that I've launched on a hop where I ended up with eight missiles that I could use. You're always wondering, "When is that damned missile going to detune on me?"'

Dosé also made some telling comments following this engagement. 'The one big mistake I made was, as soon as we got out of there, and we knew that there were MiGs behind us, we should have jettisoned our tanks, and we never did. I never thought about it'. He also said that a gun would have made a difference in the engagement, perhaps adding another kill. 'I have no doubt in the world, especially with the unimaginative defensive tactics that the MiG was using, that if I'd had an M-61 cannon, I could have hosed him right out of the sky'.

But Dosé's most interesting comments are those relating to his Topgun experience, and its effect on his flying on this day. 'During the whole engagement I felt that I had been there before. We've done so much training in this environment that you look at an aeroplane with a certain closure, and a certain airspeed, and say "Let's come this way", because that's the way you have done it before, and you know that it works'. Without question, Dosé's dissimilar ACM training at Topgun enabled him to accurately evaluate the situation, and was a major factor in the success of the mission.

When the crews returned to *Constellation* it was clear that something big had happened. Dosé and Hawkins were summoned into 'Intell', and queried on what they had hit. *Red Crown* was reporting that all available MiGs were being moved to the Hanoi/Haiphong area, and that North Vietnamese air defences were 'running wild'. The truth was that the VPAF had been hit hard, losing four MiG-21s during the early morning hours, and the Air Force, which had conducted a simultaneous strike with the Navy, had downed North Vietnam's single most important road/rail bridge, the Paul Doumer, which spanned the Red River east of Hanoi.

Dosé and Hawkins had merely helped 'stir the hive', and now the VPAF was mad, and taking to the air just in time for the day's second Alpha strike.

McDevitt and Dosé pose with their plane captain in front of 'Silver Kite 211' (BuNo 157269). Accepted by the Navy at St Louis on 5 February 1970, this aircraft served for the first year of its flying career with VF-121. Transferred to VF-92 on 12 May 1971, it subsequently deployed with the unit on its *WestPac*/Vietnam cruise aboard CVA-64 on 1 October. Used to claim VF-92's sole MiG kill of the war, on 10 May 1972, the jet returned to Miramar with the squadron on 1 July. BuNo 157269 was then transferred back to VF-121, where it remained until 12 December 1972, when it joined VF-114. Undertaking a single *WestPac* with this unit (from 23 November 1973 to 9 July 1974), BuNo 157269 rejoined VF-121 for a third time on 16 May 1975. It left the Navy F-4 training squadron for its Marine equivalent on 17 June 1976, when the fighter was sent to VMFAT-101 at Yuma. The Phantom II returned to frontline flying in June 1977 with VMFA-235, which was initially based at Yuma, but then forward-deployed to Kadena, on Okinawa, Iwakuni and Kaneohe Bay. Flown to NARF North Island on 24 October 1979, the fighter was rebuilt as an F-4S and issued to VMFA-122 at Beaufort on 7 September 1980. BuNo 157269 returned to VMFAT-101 on 11 May 1983, and was eventually flown to AMARC on 26 February 1986. Stricken from the Navy's inventory on 14 June 1993, it still languishes in storage at Davis-Monthan today (*Curt Dosé via Peter E Davies*)

Several hours after the first Alpha strike had recovered back aboard CVA-64, the aircrews of CVW-9 found themselves back in action again over the skies of North Vietnam. At approximately 1148 hrs, *Constellation* turned into wind and started launching her 32 aircraft for the strike. It would be almost 30 minutes before the strike was formed and ready to head north.

VF-96's Lt Michael J 'Matt' Connelly and RIO Lt Thomas J J Blonski (in BuNo 155769, call sign 'Showtime 106') manned one of the jets that comprised the two TAR-CAP sections supporting a major Alpha strike against the Haiphong railway sidings and the Hai Duong and Cam Pha railway bridges. The overall attacking force included strike groups from three carriers, totalling 70 strike/MiGCAP aircraft, as well as the usual supporting tankers and ECM jets.

This strike was *Constellation's* second of the day, and due to the exploits of Dosé and Hawkins, as well as the downing of the Paul Doumer Bridge, it would be opposed by more MiGs than any other mission of the war.

Also participating in this strike were Randy Cunningham and Willie Driscoll (in BuNo 155800, call sign 'Showtime 100'), and their usual wingmen, Lts Brian 'Bulldog' Grant and Jerry Sullivan. They were escorting an A-7E 'Shrike bird', flown by Lt Norman Birzer, as was Lt Steven Shoemaker and his RIO, Lt(jg) Keith V Crenshaw (in BuNo 155749, call sign 'Showtime 111'). Finally, flying MiGCAP were the XOs from both VF-92 and VF-96, Cdrs Harry L Blackburn (in BuNo 155797, call sign 'Silver Kite 212', with RIO Lt Stephen Rudloff) and Dwight Timm (BuNo 157267, call sign 'Showtime 112', flying with Lt Jim Fox).

The TARCAP F-4Js were each armed with four AIM-7E-2 Sparrows and four AIM-9G Sidewinders, plus a 600-gallon centreline tank.

The two TARCAP sections escorted the strike group to a 'feet-dry' position at the 'hourglass' rivers (south of Haiphong), then headed north up the Red River to the target area. Connelly and Blonski were off to the left of the force while the other TARCAP section was positioned to the right. As the strike group began hitting the target, the strike leader, CVW-9 CAG Cdr Lowell 'Gus' Eggert, called 'Play ball! Play ball!' At once, each TARCAP section made a level cross-turn, passing the other section in combat-spread. Connelly and his wing headed south, establishing a barrier against MiGs from Bai Thuong. They soon began to receive MiG calls from *Red Crown*.

The first call Connelly heard was from an A-7 pilot screaming that there were MiGs on his tail, and for somebody to come and get them off. The pilot was so excited that he neglected to give his position, and Connelly had to radio, 'Where are you?' Looking down, he saw an A-7 (flown by Lt Birzer) at his 'three o'clock', low, at about three nautical miles, with two MiG-17s right behind it. The lead MiG was firing 37 mm rounds at the Corsair II but was not pulling lead.

Connelly called 'Tally-ho' and then commanded a 6G break turn to engage the bandits. As soon as he pulled G, his RIO Blonski hollered 'We just lost the damned radar! We've got a black scope'. Connelly tried desperately to maintain visual contact with the MiGs, and eventually lost his wingman – the two remained separated throughout the rest of the engagement. Apparently having seen Connelly roll in, MiG 2 immediately broke to the right.

The pilot of 'Showtime 106' continued to pursue the lead MiG, sliding into a position about 8000 ft behind it and 30 degrees angle-off. Birzer's A-7 then started to roll wings-level, with the MiG right behind it. Although Connelly felt he was out of the firing envelope for his Sidewinders, he decided 'I've got to shoot now to get that guy off Birzer's tail', and he squeezed the trigger. The AIM-9 launched with good tone, but it didn't seem to guide. The MiG 'driver' must have seen it coming and broke hard enough to nearly meet the F-4 head-on.

Using the same kind of hand gestures as those employed by Curt Dosé in the photograph seen on page 34, VF-96's Lt 'Matt' Connelly shows his squadronmates exactly how he destroyed two MiG-17s in quick succession over Hai Duong. Looking on is his RIO, Lt Thomas Blonski (*via Robert F Dorr*)

Connelly then came right back into the MiG and found himself at the bottom of a large dogfight with VPAF jets 'all over the place'. He offers his thoughts on the engagement that followed;

'To come back and try to reconstruct what followed after that on a blackboard is impossible. I don't even know if the first MiG I shot down was the same guy that I initially shot at. I don't think it was, but everything was so confusing, and there were so damned many of them! They were all over the place! If you were chasing one, and looked over and saw another one that was less angle-off, and you had less degrees to pull to get at his "six", you just went after him.

'The whole thing transpired at about 7000 ft or so. I had enough energy to maintain the bottom of the fight, and control it pretty well. I didn't want to go up with the other F-4s because I could pick the MiGs up easily. They were always about 1000 ft above me when I picked them up, and I had plenty of altitude over the ground, so I wasn't worrying about it that much.'

After turning back into the lead bogey and finding a sky full of MiGs (as many as 20), Connelly, now in full afterburner, locked his eyes onto another MiG-17 (MiG 3), which was in a right turn at about 300 knots. The MiG's pilot apparently did not see Connelly, who was then slightly off of his tail and manoeuvring. Realising that he was closing too fast, Connelly pulled the power back to idle and popped his speed brakes.

As MiG 3 started to roll wings-level, Connelly brought the speed brakes back in, drifting in behind his target. Obtaining a good tone, he squeezed the trigger, loosing an AIM-9 off the rails and sending it straight up the MiG's tailpipe. The VPAF jet exploded in a huge ball of fire. Although he did not realise it until after he returned to the carrier, Connelly must have fired this missile just seconds after deciding to retract the speed brakes, for the weapon's exhaust burned a hole in his left brake!

Connelly remembers that the MiGs seemed to 'jump on aircraft that were arcing around the sky'. He was not really threatened because he was either chasing a MiG or rapidly switching from one to another. Picking up another MiG-17 (MiG 4) in a right turn, Connelly made an attack similar to the one which had resulted in his first kill.

As he and Blonski started drifting towards its 'six o'clock', MiG 4 reversed left, putting Connelly on the inside of its turn. Then, apparently not seeing the F-4, the MiG rolled out to a wings-level position. 'I had a really good tone', Connelly said, 'and I took my time because I only had three Sidewinders (all that had been loaded). I had wasted the first one. The second worked, and I really wanted to make the third one work too'.

At about 4000-5000 ft, Connelly triggered another missile, but just as he fired the tone dropped off. The AIM-9 departed, made a corkscrew, and detonated alongside the MiG. Connelly thought that he had missed, but his RIO Blonski called, 'Wait a minute, his tail's gone'. Smoke then started streaming from the aeroplane, and the MiG rolled left and the pilot ejected.

An F-4 passed less than 1000 ft over the top of Connelly while he was watching MiG 4. The next thing he saw was a MiG-17 (MiG 5) sitting about 30 ft out at his 'nine o'clock'. This MiG was almost flying wing on Connelly, with both aircraft at 220 knots. 'He was co-speed and I was at 220 knots', Connelly noted. 'I thought, "You almost had your ass shot off!" I don't know what the hell I was doing or how we got that way. If you lined up ten "Gomers" tomorrow, I could recognise that SOB. He wasn't flying with an oxygen mask. I was looking at him and he was looking at me'.

To counter the VPAF pilot, Connelly performed a slow-speed roll over the top of MiG 5, which put it in his 'three o'clock'. He felt confident that he could perform a rolling scissors and thought 'That's the only thing I can do right now'. MiG 5 followed him through the manoeuvre, but then for no apparent reason its pilot dumped the nose and disengaged. Connelly noted, 'He (MiG 5) wouldn't have had to do too much of anything if he had continued his slow fight until he got behind and started to pepper us. For the life of me I can't figure out why he broke off'.

Despite having fired all of his Sidewinders, and with his radar unserviceable (leaving him without the ability to employ his four Sparrow missiles), Connelly nevertheless set off in pursuit of two more MiG-17s (MiGs 6 and 7). 'I used the old philosophy "it's easier for me to chase them than to have one of them behind me". I chased one of them (MiG 6) around for a while, and he was pulling pretty hard. He finally dropped his nose and started diving for the deck.

'I thought he was going to go home, so we started to make a turn towards the beach. Then another one (MiG 7) flew right in front of me. He was turning to the left and I just followed him. He did the same thing as the other one, and I don't think he ever saw me. I was right behind him, and just chasing him around. I could have been in an excellent gun position – all I would have had to do was add a little more power and catch them'.

Most of the aircraft were starting to exit the area, so Connelly made another full-circle sweep before heading out. As he checked the area, he saw an F-4 (belonging to Cunningham and Driscoll) with a MiG-17 (MiG 8) pulling up below him. Connelly called, 'F-4 heading 180 degrees. You've got a MiG-17 coming up behind you. Unload, full 'burner – you can outrun him'. But the F-4 did not respond. Connelly started pulling his nose towards MiG 8 and selected radar as he repeated the call. Cunningham finally heard Connelly's warnings and unloaded in full afterburner.

At a distance of about two nautical miles, and a 20-degree aspect angle, Connelly put his pipper on MiG 8. With his radar scope still black, but the missile select lights on, he squeezed the trigger, hoping to force the MiG to break off its attack. 'I was really appalled at the missile', Connelly later remarked. 'Normally a Sparrow comes out and starts doing ballistic trajectories. This one came off and started going right at him. The trouble is, before the Sparrow got to the guy I pulled my nose away from him and headed for "feet-wet". The second that the thing came off the rail and travelled a hundred yards, the MiG just snapped right off Cunningham's F-4. All of a sudden the guy was nose down, diving away, and we had resumed our heading out towards the beach'.

Unfortunately, the Sparrow passed right over the MiG as it turned to disengage and missed. Connelly then egressed and headed back to the carrier. He later added, 'An interesting side note was the fact that there was plenty of gas (tankers) in the air but we couldn't find it. We stayed on strike frequency for a while and got the run around. We decide, "That's not going to work", and went to Marshall, and they said, "Standby". Finally, we went to Tower and he said "We've got a tanker I'm launching two right now"'.

By then Connelly was within 30 nautical miles of the ship, and he realised that he had enough fuel to make it. He landed with just 700 lbs remaining in his tanks.

Connelly told the *Red Baron* interviewers that 'Neither of the MiGs manoeuvred while the missiles were in flight. Neither had a wingman. They were out there by themselves. Every guy we engaged was single, aside from the first two'.

In contrast, the American crews were much better trained and disciplined. 'The most significant thing was the section integrity. Sections were made and dissolved in seconds. We maintained mutual support. The whole fight was contained within about a four-mile area, and you could see the other black-nose aeroplanes. You'd see a guy with a MiG behind him, and you would come on the radio and say, "Keep pulling to port". I heard a lot of that on the radio. Sections were made and dissolved in just seconds with that kind of quick mutual support'.

A three-ship formation of F-4Js from the 'Black Falcons' release their Mk 82 bombs (six apiece) over North Vietnam in the spring of 1972. Closest to the camera is CAG jet BuNo 155800 – a future triple MiG killer (*via Peter E Davies*)

Connelly says that the MiG's camouflage helped the VPAF pilots escape once they committed to disengaging. 'When the MiGs disengage, they all dump their noses and go right down to the deck. That damned camouflage – you get them in that rice paddy and you lose them. You can have them locked up visually, but as soon as they get down there in those rice paddies, you can't see them'.

As to the F-4's lack of guns, Connelly also said, 'There's no doubt in my mind that if we had had gas and guns, we probably would have bagged five that day. It would have been easy'. Blonski reiterated this, stating that 'To have a fighter without a gun is just asinine'.

The RIO said of the engagement, 'If all the MiG "drivers" that day had the benefit of the training that we've had, and if they had had a chance to fly against an aeroplane comparable to the F-4, it might have been disastrous, because we made mistakes. We've never experienced that many MiGs in a confined area at one time'. Blonski also said that the North Vietnamese had 'set up a flak trap that bagged one F-4 before the MiGs arrived. He (Cdr Blackburn) flew into their flak trap and was blown out of the sky. He was really set up for it'.

But Connelly and Blonski's kills were just the beginning of the fight.

Two of the VF-96 crews participating in this second mission were tasked with providing flak-suppression for CVW-9's strike on the Hai Duong marshalling yard south-east of Hanoi. Armed with Rockeye cluster bomb units (fitted to bulky triple ejector racks), four AIM-9 Sidewinders and two AIM-7 Sparrows, the jets were crewed by Randy Cunningham and Willie Driscoll, as lead, and Brian Grant and Jerry Sullivan in the wing slot.

During their ingress to the target area, the Phantom II crews encountered two SAMs and heavy AAA. Fortunately, neither missile tracked well, and the mission proceeded normally until the A-6s of the strike package missed the target due to overcast skies and had to be called back. In the resulting confusion, all of the strike aircraft ended up making their bombing runs from the same direction.

Cunningham later commented, 'The mistake that everybody made was that their runs were all from west to east, and they looked like a line of ants

Arguably the most famous Navy Phantom II of them all, 'Showtime 100' is seen patrolling over the Gulf of Tonkin on 29 March 1972. BuNo 155800 was accepted by the Navy at St Louis on 17 October 1968 and issued new to VF-96 two days later. One of the first F-4Js sent to the unit in place of its war-weary B-models, the fighter participated in its first war cruise, aboard USS *Enterprise* (CVAN-65) between 6 January and 2 July 1969. BuNo 155800 ventured to sea once again with VF-96 aboard USS *America* (CVA-66) on 10 April 1970, when CVW-9 conducted a Vietnam cruise with the Atlantic Fleet carrier that lasted until 22 December. The jet's third *WestPac*/Vietnam deployment commenced on 1 October 1971, aboard the *Constellation*. As with its previous two cruises, BuNo 155800 was marked up as VF-96's CAG jet. On 10 May 1972, 'Duke' Cunningham and 'Willie' Driscoll used 'Showtime 100' to down three MiG-17s, thus making them the first American aces of the Vietnam conflict. Later in the mission the aircraft was badly damaged by a SAM which exploded beneath the fighter, and the crew was forced to eject just beyond the North Vietnamese coastline when BuNo 155800's hydraulic systems failed. It had completed 1813 flight hours up until its final, historic, sortie (*via Robert F Dorr*)

going down a hill. One F-4, right across the circle from my wingman and I, circled around to the north following the same flight path as the A-6s and A-7s after they had rolled in. An 85 mm cannon barrage hit him (Cdr Blackburn). Flying in the same airspace just vacated by previous aeroplanes not only cost him his life and caused his RIO (Steve Rudloff) to become a PoW, but also resulted in his wingman (Rod Dilworth and Gerry Hill) being hit by the same barrage and losing an engine'.

Although the day was clear and there was AAA all over the sky, Cunningham and Grant could not pick up muzzle flashes to pin-point the gun locations for targeting with their Rockeyes. This left them with little option but to switch from the flak-suppression role and go after their secondary target – a long red storage building. A SAM was launched at them during their attack, but after a small break it did not track, and the Phantom IIs continued in on their run.

Cunningham had pulled off and rolled back right to observe his Rockeye 'walking' through the target when Grant called, '"Duke", you've got MiG-17s at "seven o'clock"'. Flying at a speed of just 380 knots, Cunningham quickly reversed and saw three MiG-17s (MiGs 1, 2 and 3) closing rapidly, about 3000 ft away. In Cunningham's words, 'My instinctive reaction was to break into the MiGs, but I knew that if I did, they would rendezvous on me. I thought, "I'm slow, so I don't have that many possibilities. I can't go up, and to use the MiG-17 disengagement manoeuvre when he's got closure is asinine. He'll just run right up my tailpipe"'.

Cunningham then put his nose low, stood on the rudder pedals and pulled back on the stick. The first MiG (MiG 1) overshot slightly under and in front of him. Stabbing his right rudder pedal to the floor, he reversed back to the right, then began a reversal.

'Just as I picked him (MiG 1) up', Cunningham later related, 'his two wingmen pitched up and rolled in on me. The MiG-17 "driver" (MiG 1) didn't keep any angle-off, and it was a zero-deflection shot. His tailpipe was sitting right there in front of me. He was still in afterburner, and he had his nose down, which allowed me to accelerate. As I reversed, I selected 'burner, nosed down and got a tone while I was unloading. I was pushing forward-stick and squeezing the trigger at the same time. The missile hit him, and this was one of the few MiGs that I had hit that only had little pieces knocked off. The MiG went out of control and smashed into the ground.

Seen in more peaceful surrounds at NAS Quonset Point, Rhode Island, in the summer of 1971, a recently-resprayed 'Showtime 100' was visiting the east coast air station as a participant in its base open house (*via Robert F Dorr*)

Hoping to drag the two MiGs in front of Grant's F-4, Cunningham was surprised to hear his wingman call, 'I can't help you, One'. Cunningham looked back and saw four more MiG-17s attacking Grant. 'At this point', Cunningham related, 'our mutual support degraded a little bit'. Using a disengagement manoeuvre, he pulled out just ahead of the two MiGs. Grant, too, also used this manoeuvre, and was quickly back on Cunningham's wing.

Both pilots had now dropped their centreline tanks. The triple ejector racks, however, were a different story. Cunningham would have liked to jettison them to reduce drag, but if they went, so did the remaining Sidewinders, which were being carried on the same weapons stations.

Cunningham called, 'Okay, cross-turn, Two. We're going back in'. They now had good airspeed, and were about 5000 ft above the fight. As they returned, Cunningham saw three F-4s in a 350-knot defensive wheel (Lufbery) with eight MiG-17s. 'Everything was in slow motion', he recalled. 'On one side you'd see MiG-19s climbing, and over there you'd see a MiG-17 going down in flames. In slow motion you'd see F-4s zooming and you'd see MiGs after them. I thought something was the matter with me. At that point in the fight I was probably very vulnerable to something coming up my "six o'clock".

Then Cunningham saw four more MiG-17s join in the Lufbery for a total of twelve, with four MiG-21s above the fight not engaged. There were also two MiG-19s about three nautical miles off his right wing.

Cunningham intended to make a supersonic pass through the Lufbery. 'I'm engaged, you're free', he called as he rolled in. Grant replied, 'One. I'm caught again'. Looking back, he saw more MiG-17s swarming all over his wingman – these were not part of the 12 in the Lufbery. 'I don't know where they came from', Cunningham remarked, 'but there were enough MiGs for everybody. That's the point where you realise there's really not a tooth fairy!'

At about the same time Grant called that he was engaged, another VF-96 jet in a left turn in the Lufbery came belly-up to Cunningham. The Phantom II was being flown by XO Dwight Timm (with RIO Jim Fox) at about 350 knots, and he had a MiG-17 firing from 3000 ft behind him, a MiG-21 about 4500 ft back on the inside of his turn and a second MiG-17 (MiG 4) 300 ft away from him on his belly side. Cunningham called, '"Showtime", reverse starboard', but Timm did not see MiG 4 and continued his turn. Finally, Cunningham shouted, 'Turn your aircraft and unload or you'll be dead'. At this call, Dwight Timm reversed, saw MiG 4, unloaded and started accelerating away – Cunningham then positioned for a Sidewinder tone.

He was trying to stay in a lag-pursuit position on MiG 4, which was chasing Timm, when the two MiG-19s at his 'three o'clock' rolled in on him. There were also four MiG-17s behind Cunningham on the in side of his turn and four MiG-21s 5000 ft overhead. He described the subsequent events;

'The MiG-17s behind us were dropping back, but every time Timm would arc they would rendezvous on me. At one time they got to about 2000 ft away. The MiG-17s would close, and I'd have to go back to the lag-pursuit position at 500 knots and pull up. At this time the MiG-19s rolled in on us and I broke up hard into them, which actually helped me because it resulted in a lag-pursuit roll to the outside of the MiG-17 (MiG 4).'

Timm and Fox started to use the disengagement manoeuvre, but for some reason the XO put the G back in and the MiG-17 rendezvoused on him again. As Cunningham continued to manoeuvre into position on MiG 4, the MiG-19s went out to his 'six o'clock' and pulled their noses up into a loop, tangent to his circle. He never saw them again. Cunningham now had three MiG-17s ahead and four behind him, four MiG-21s about 5000 ft above and the two MiG-19s that had just disappeared at his 'three o'clock'.

'We were lucky after this', he continued. 'Timm's F-4 unloaded again and walked away from the MiG-17s. The MiG-21 (that was inside of the XO's turn) broke off for some reason and I never saw him again'.

Cunningham now had MiG 4, which was in afterburner, centred in his windscreen, with a good tone on his AIM-9G. As soon as Cdr Timm came out of 'burner, Cunningham squeezed the trigger. The Sidewinder tracked to the MiG and detonated. 'I almost hit the pilot', he recalled. 'He had on little Gomer goggles and a little Gomer hat, and he had boots laced up to the knees. The guy didn't even wave'.

Following his second kill of the day, Cunningham looked around and saw MiGs everywhere, but did not see any other friendlies. He therefore started to egress and head for the carrier. As Cunningham left, he picked up a dot on the horizon about 20 degrees to the right, and quickly identified it as a MiG-17 (MiG 5). He decided to play a game of chicken with the MiG, as he had often done to rattle other pilots at Miramar, and turned into it. As the two closed head-on, the MiG started firing.

'It didn't even dawn on me that he was going to shoot at me', Cunningham later recalled. 'It was something I'd practised and practised against A-4s, and there's a saying "You fight like you train". I'd made a mistake in not visualising the actual weapons capability that the MiG had in that situation because the A-4s I flew against didn't have guns. So I smartly moved out to the side and he still kept shooting short bursts. The 23 mm cannon shoots out a flame about a yard long. No exaggeration – it's scary'.

Cunningham still had plenty of fuel (an unusual situation in an F-4), and he decided to engage the MiG-17. 'All the other MiGs that I saw would either run or they'd turn horizontally – they were all plumbers. So, when I met him (MiG 5) I pitched straight up. I was going to get another easy kill and then bug out. I expected to see him in the horizontal, running, about three miles away. As I rolled back up and started bringing my head back, looking for the horizon, what I least expected to see was the MiG canopy-to-canopy with me, but there he was, about 400 or 500 ft away from me, going straight up'.

A short burst from the MiG forced Cunningham to quarter-turn out of the plane of fire. He then pulled towards the MiG's 'six o'clock' and they entered a rolling scissors manoeuvre. 'I got the advantage when he put his nose down for airspeed', Cunningham stated. 'As soon as his nose went low, I started putting my nose down. All of a sudden his nose came up so fast it was amazing. As my nose went down, I went out a little bit in front. The fight was going advantage-disadvantage, and then it started going disadvantage-disadvantage'.

More 'talking hands', as 'Randy' Cunningham 'holds court' in the VF-96 ready room at 1920 hrs on the evening of 10 May. Just a few hours earlier, he and RIO 'Willie' Driscoll had been fished out of the Gulf of Tonkin by a SAR HH-3A and flown to the Marine helicopter assault ship USS *Okinawa* (LPH-3). From there, they had been transferred back to the 'Connie' by a Marine Corps CH-46. Having downed three MiG-17s in eight minutes to 'make ace', and then been shot down by a SAM, Cunningham certainly had a few tales to tell! The pilot at the extreme right of the photograph, with his face turned towards 'Duke' Cunningham, is Cdr Dwight Timm, XO of VF-96 (*via Robert F Dorr*)

Flying straight up in the vertical, Cunningham disengaged from the rolling scissors. When the MiG-17 had its nose high, he kicked rudder, pulled to the MiG's 'six o'clock' and gained separation, then he pitched back into the fight. 'I didn't have the knots', Cunningham said, referring to his speed, 'and I almost got bagged – he rendezvoused on me'. The American again unloaded and picked up a good airspeed, before turning once more into the MiG.

'I pulled it through as hard as I could, but it was to the point that I couldn't meet him head-on. What really surprised me was that little MiG-17 zoomed with me up there. I expected his nose to fall off, but it didn't. It ended in a carbon copy of the first engagement – a rolling scissors – but again I disengaged in the same manner.'

Each time Cunningham went out in front, the MiG's cannon would fire. 'I'm not going out in front this time', Cunningham told Driscoll. 'This time we're going to get where I know I can at least meet him head-on'. Obtaining the energy level he desired, Cunningham zoomed and the MiG once again went into the vertical with him. Then, chopping his throttles, he went to idle power with speed brakes extended.

Cunningham continues. 'Here I am, sitting behind a MiG-17, nose up. As soon as I saw relative motion stop, I went back into full 'burner and locked about 1000 ft behind him, but he would hold angle-off. I was on the rudders, just sitting, and I thought, "Boy, what a stupid decision you just made. You're really in great shape, 1000 ft behind a MiG-17, 170 knots, slowing". The only thing is, I always had the feeling that I could disengage any time I wanted to'.

The MiG-17 had been operating in afterburner for about five minutes. and was evidently now down to a critical fuel state because he tried to disengage and made a run for Kep. The VPAF jet did a slow-speed reversal, went almost 45 degrees nose down and started rocking his wings as if he had lost sight of Cunningham. As he headed towards Kep, the MiG stopped wing-rocking and dived for the deck.

'I guess he thought he could outrun me', said Cunningham. 'I started pushing forward on the stick, trying not to bury the nose, and I actually had to stand on the rudder a little bit to hold the nose up. I unloaded and squeezed the trigger as I got the tone. It knocked off a little piece of the tail but didn't alter his flightpath at all, and I thought he was going to get away. He was still running. I followed him down and started to squeeze again when a little fire erupted'. Cunningham continued to watch as the MiG descended into the ground. No ejection was seen.

Whilst following the fleeing MiG, four other MiG-17s and a single MiG-21 had fallen in behind 'Showtime 100'. The MiG-17s were about a mile astern, with the MiG-21 some distance further back. Cunningham was warned of this new threat by fellow VF-96 pilot Lt Michael J 'Matt' Connelly. On his advice, Cunningham went to afterburner and accelerated away from the MiG-17 behind him, then pitched up into another MiG-17 which was attacking him from 'two o'clock'. At this point Connelly fired an AIM-7E-2 into the MiGs and they scattered, departing the area.

As Cunningham and Driscoll were egressing, they heard SAM calls. The pilot remembers looking to his right and seeing a missile. However, just as he started to turn, the missile went off about 500 ft above him – the VPAF have maintained that 'Showtime 100' was hit by an Atoll missile fired by a MiG-21, as was the VF-92 jet of Blackburn and Rudloff. The F-4 shuddered a little, but all gauges appeared normal and Cunningham continued his climb out. At 25,000 ft, the aircraft gave a hard pitch to the left and the pilot realised that he had lost both the utility system and the PC-1 hydraulic system, with PC-2 starting to fluctuate.

'I came out of 'burner and left it at 100 per cent, and then the nose went straight up on me. It was not very violent though – it just started a climb, and I pushed the stick full forward, but nothing happened. I remember kicking bottom rudder and I thought, "Okay, roll this SOB out". We started rolling, and the thought went through my mind not to bury the nose because I'd never get it out with rudder. As soon as the nose started approaching the horizon, I stood on the opposite rudder and tried to slice

Clutching their flight gear and helmets, 'Randy' Cunningham and 'Willie' Driscoll return to CVA-64 minus 'Showtime 100'. Note that Driscoll seems to have lost his flying boots during his hasty evacuation of his crippled jet. Minutes after this photograph was taken, Cunningham and Driscoll were surrounded by well-wishers. 'Everyone knew we had gotten three MiGs to become aces, but the statement that moved us the most was made by one of the enlisted troops. He walked up to me and said, "Mr Cunningham, we are glad you shot down three MiGs today and became aces, but we're even happier that you're back with us!" That statement really brought home to me the importance of the team effort that allowed us to shoot down those MiGs. Every one of the men on the "Connie" deserves credit for our victories. Their efforts made them possible', 'Duke' Cunningham later said (*via Robert F Dorr*)

the nose through. Once I had got the right wing up, I stood on the right rudder and got the nose climbing again. It sounds smooth, but it was violent as hell'.

About this time Willie Driscoll looked out and said 'We're on fire'. Cunningham recalled, 'We lost a wing tip, and luckily the fire had blown our radios too. I'm glad now, because on the tape you can hear guys screaming at us to eject. The aeroplane was on fire, part of the wing was missing, and they said it looked like a blow torch going through the sky. The cockpits were all right. There wasn't any smoke – there wasn't anything except a lot of anticipation. We kept rolling the aeroplane for some 15 miles like that'.

Soon after Cunningham went 'feet-wet' the utility system failed completely and the aircraft entered a spin. Both crew members ejected successfully and were recovered from the sea by two of the three HH-3As from HC-7 that had been waiting off the coast, performing the Combat Search and Rescue role. They were flown back to USS *Okinawa* (LPH-3), and then onto the *Constellation* by a Marine Corps CH-46 later that same day.

Following the events of 10 May, Randy Cunningham discussed the engagement with *Red Baron* investigators;

'Probably the most important thing that came out of the whole fight was that if we had had a gun in the aeroplane, I would have three more MiGs today. We flew up behind three MiG-17s flying straight and level, and filled the windscreen full of MiG before we had to pitch off. We couldn't manoeuvre because of MiGs chasing us, and couldn't shoot because we were inside minimum (missile) range.'

MORE KILLS FOR VF-96

The final MiG kill credited to VF-96 on 10 May fell to ex-*Blue Angels* pilot Lt Steven Shoemaker and his RIO, Lt(jg) Keith V Crenshaw (in BuNo 155749, call sign 'Showtime 111'). Like Cunningham and Driscoll, they were assigned as an escort for the A-7E *Iron Hand* aircraft flown by Lt Norman Birzer, which was in turn providing ECM protection for the Alpha strike on the Hai Duong marshalling yards.

The mixed section headed incountry to the left of the strike group, towards the bottom tip of the 'hourglass' rivers, then turned north and headed for the target area. The section was operating at an altitude of 12,000-14,000 ft, and cruising at about 350 knots, with Shoemaker and Crenshaw escorting from a modified wing position on the A-7. Shoemaker weaved back and forth between 1000 and 1500 ft above Birzer, covering his own 'six o'clock', and maintaining sufficient speed to keep the big fighter manoeuvrable.

Looking every inch the fighter ace in his dress whites, an immaculately groomed Lt 'Randy' Cunningham is interviewed by the world's press in Saigon on 11 May 1972. Such news conferences were dubbed the 'Five O'Clock Follies' by the naval crews that participated in them (*via Peter Mersky*)

The Honourable John W Warner, Secretary of the Navy, pins the Navy Cross on Lt(jg) 'Willie' Driscoll at NAS Miramar on 14 October 1972. Standing to the right of Driscoll, already wearing his medal, is Lt 'Randy' Cunningham. This presentation took place during the establishment ceremony for the Navy's first two F-14 Tomcat units, VF-1 and VF-2 (*via Peter Mersky*)

About halfway to Hai Duong, the A-7 pilot pre-emptively fired an AGM-45 Shrike towards a SAM site located south of Hanoi. The firing represented a new tactic for the Americans, for the North Vietnamese had been firing SAMs without guidance, then turning on their radars at the last minute. This tactic reduced the opportunity for the Shrikes, which were being launched in direct support of the strike force.

As a result of this change made by the communists, the Navy had adopted a 'nav-loft' tactic, which meant that the Shrikes would be launched into an area of probable SAM activity from about 25 miles out, and, crucially, before the missile controller began transmitting. When the radar did come on, the Shrike was ready to pounce.

As Birzer manoeuvred the A-7 to launch his second Shrike, the section heard *Red Crown* call, 'Bandits, *Bullseye*, 030 degrees, 26 miles, heading 220 degrees, altitude unknown'. The section was at 090 degrees at 30 nautical miles from *Bullseye* (Hanoi) at the time, and it turned north-east to head for a second SAM site. Moments later someone yelled, 'Hey, there's MiGs on the strike group. There's MiGs attacking the strike group'.

Since the MiGs were located at his 'six', Shoemaker called for the section to come left and head for the strike group. If the MiGs should attack, he wanted them to come at the section's front, not its tail. Shoemaker takes up the story;

'I turned him (the A-7) left, and he said, 'Okay, I've got an F-4 at my "two o'clock", and I replied "No sweat. That's me". That's the last time I saw the A-7, because as I looked up I saw a MiG coming our way. I don't know what happened to the A-7. He got the hell out and never said anything. I had just started heading towards the strike group, and it was really getting wild then. About this time another A-7 pilot came up and yelled, "I got one on my ass". He was screaming "Somebody get that SOB off of me". The MiG-17 chased him all the way to the coastline, and he was screaming all the way!'

The MiG-17 passed to the left of Shoemaker, about 2000 ft out, level, and kept going – no attempt was made by either aircraft to attack. The next thing Shoemaker saw was a large dogfight involving Connelly/Blonski and Cunningham/Driscoll. RIO Crenshaw said of the distant dogfight, 'Man, it was a massive "hassle". It was as if someone said, "I'll meet you over San Clemente (an island off San Diego over which much West Coast fighter training took place) with my six F-4s and you get your eight F-8s out here and we will have at it". Aeroplanes going up and around, missiles going off and 'chutes in the air. I saw 'chutes and heard beepers. It was mass confusion'.

Shoemaker also talked about his view of the 'furball'. 'My main thought was, "God, I'm out here alone and I don't have a 'wingy' protecting 'my six'", so I had my RIO turn around. He was nearly unstrapped looking over that ejection seat, and I was really moving the aeroplane. I figured that with as many MiGs as there were flying around, chances were that I would surely fly in front of one of them. It really made me nervous. I didn't think I needed to coax my RIO to look around behind us because it was his rear end on the line too'.

The next thing that caught Shoemaker's attention was an F-4 with a MiG-17 'camped on its six', with another F-4 chasing the MiG with

The last kill to be credited to VF-96 on 10 May was claimed by ex-*Blue Angel* Lt Steven Shoemaker and Lt(jg) Keith Crenshaw. Although they actually downed their MiG-17 four minutes prior to Cunningham and Driscoll 'bagging' their third kill of the mission, the crew of 'Showtime 111' did not see their MiG either being struck by the Sidewinder that they had fired, or the stricken jet hit the ground. 'We came on this MiG-17 to the south-west of the "furball" over Hai Duong. He appeared in front of us, and he seemed to be trying to get out of the fight. We didn't make any big turn. We just dived on him, and I heard "Shoe" call, "We got good tone", then he fired the Sidewinder. After that we had to pull up, as we were getting too close to the ground. We lost sight of both the missile and the MiG. We got some altitude then rolled over, and on the ground was what was obviously an aeroplane burning, giving off thick black greasy smoke', explained RIO Crenshaw. Although initially listed as a probable, this MiG-17 was subsequently credited to the crew as a confirmed kill. Keith Crenshaw had not seen a MiG 'in the flesh' up until this sortie. 'Previously, we had agreed that if we hassled with MiGs I would search aft of the wing line and "Shoe" would search forward of it. I had been looking behind, and one of the vivid memories I have of that fight is the sight of a canopy as a MiG-17 suddenly appeared and rolled over the top of us! It was very close, about 500 ft away – the first MiG I had ever seen. I said, "Er, 'Shoe', there's a MiG just gone over the top of us . . ." He replied, "Jesus, Keith, look around!" I glanced forward and there were MiGs all over the place, two of them in flames. We went whipping by a guy swinging on a parachute' (*via Peter Mersky*)

80-90 degrees angle-off. He remembers thinking, 'That poor SOB is going to get killed'. As Shoemaker watched, the F-4 swung around in front of him, with the MiG following behind, and firing.

'I'll just "hose" one off', Shoemaker thought, 'and scare the hell out of that MiG driver. If nothing else, hopefully he will make a mistake and the other F-4 can get into position for a good shot'. Shoemaker rolled out, put his pipper on the MiG and fired a Sidewinder from about 90 degrees angle-off, without tone, from a range of about 1500 ft. The missile went over the top of the MiG's left wing, about halfway between the wing tip and the wing root. 'I don't even know whether my missile had any effect on the MiG', Shoemaker later said of the launch.

'I didn't have a valid shot. I wanted to scare him and make him break off, or make a mistake. The next thing that happened was that I almost had a mid-air with the second F-4! He was chasing that guy and I was watching where the missile went when he pulled right up in front of me. I broke left, with them still in their happy little gaggle. I figured I'd better get out of there – they could handle it by themselves. I wasn't going to get involved in that one again. I guess they got rid of him right after that'.

Shoemaker then broke off and made a full circle turn, during which he saw two square 'chutes with red circles on them, heard beepers going off and watched another F-4 (probably Connelly and Blonski) down a

MiG with a missile. Worried about a MiG sneaking up behind him, Shoemaker talked continually to his RIO Crenshaw, and repeatedly asked, 'How's our "Six"?'

Heading out at 8000 ft, Shoemaker saw two F-4s egressing, the second in trail with the first, about 2-3 nautical miles south-west of the target area. A MiG-17 (MiG 3) was 3000-4000 ft behind them, low, at their 'six' position. Before Shoemaker could transmit a warning, the MiG started an easy left turn, 20-30 degree angle of bank. Shoemaker headed for the MiG and flew over it with a separation distance of some 2000 ft. When the VPAF jet started descending, he began spiralling down in hot pursuit. Shoemaker describes what happened next;

'We were descending all the time. I probably started at 5000 or 6000 ft, and it seemed to me we went around twice, or maybe a turn-and-a-half. He (MiG 3) wasn't diving for the deck. He was spiralling straight down, over a point, and I just fell in behind him. I don't think he ever saw me. I wasn't really pulling hard to get there, but was diving with my nose about 300 degrees below the horizon. I arrived at a position on him – about 10-20 degrees off, pipper on him, good tone, inside his turn about 2000 ft back – and I fired.

'He was then at a height of about 1000 ft, and I was at 1500-2000 ft. The missile came off the rail and I broke hard to starboard to clear my "six". I'd been concentrating on getting behind this guy, and somebody could have easily slipped up behind me, as I was in a steady turn. I rolled it back to the left again, but the MiG was gone. Then I looked at the ground right down below me and could see black smoke. Right then my RIO yelled, "We've got a MiG at our 'eight o'clock'". I rolled out and a MiG-17 (MiG 4) slid over to my "eight o'clock", about 2000 ft away'.

In what must have been a strange moment of war, the two pilots stared at each other for a few seconds. Then, after dipping its left wing as it was going to turn away, the MiG started rolling towards Shoemaker. He then rolled out, unloaded, hit afterburner and, with negative-G, immediately started walking away.

As Shoemaker recalls, 'The thing that really struck me about this engagement is that they always said that the MiG-17 had a slow roll-rate, but this guy was rolling so slowly it was ridiculous. The guy started rolling really slowly, and got his nose up a little bit. I was in 'burner, going like a streak, well out of gun range. We walked away from him like a Cadillac going away from a Volkswagen.'

Although Shoemaker and Crenshaw separated from the MiG without difficulty, during the engagement the crew had lost all of its compass systems except the 'whiskey' compass.

Shoemaker was now down to a low fuel state, and he had to disengage. He describes his conclusion of the engagement, 'I ended up going every which way. Did you ever try to make yourself fly straight and level to read the wet compass knowing that you're the last guy in there? I had a SAM shot at me at 500 ft when I was heading towards Haiphong, trying to find my way out of there. I finally ended up finding one of the "hourglass" rivers, and I followed it out and went "feet-wet" with about 800 lbs of fuel left. I think trying to get out of there was almost more interesting than the MiG engagement'. After successfully egressing the area, the crew returned to their carrier without further incident.

Shoemaker said that during the engagement he 'didn't see any two MiGs that looked like they were together. They were all over the place'. Moreover, the MiG pilots seemed to be ill-suited to flying tactically. 'Almost all the MiGs that I saw were in a tight turn, on the inside, going towards someone's "six", and all horizontal'. He added, 'I sure wouldn't have any instincts if all I flew were intercept hops. If all you ever did was turn horizontally, that's all you're going to be able to do'.

'SCREAMING EAGLE 111'

Constellation's Phantom IIs were not the only Navy F-4s battling MiGs on 10 May. Concurrent with the VF-92 and VF-96 engagements, F-4Bs from *Coral Sea's* VF-51 were flying MiGCAP support for a major Alpha strike on the Hai Duong Railway Bridge between Haiphong and Hanoi.

Although the fighters' pre-planned station was to have been over Phantom Ridge, north-east of Haiphong, *Red Crown* (on this occasion their controller was Radarman First Class Nalwalker) assigned them to a CAP station just south of Haiphong.

Flying as wing to Lt Cdr Chuck Schroeder (and his RIO, Lt(jg) Dale Arends), Lt Kenneth L 'Ragin Cajun' Cannon and RIO Lt Roy A 'Bud' Morris Jr (in BuNo 151398, call sign 'Screaming Eagle 111') held on their assigned station at 10,000 ft, 'feet-wet'. During their orbit, *Red Crown* moved the location. 'Your new CAP station is 280 degrees at 60 miles', which repositioned them at a point about 20 nautical miles south of Hanoi.

As the Phantom IIs headed 280 degrees, they started a descent to just 100-200 ft. Cannon related, 'Our thoughts were that we could either dodge SAMs or look for MiG, and we chose to look for MiGs down low. We decided to get down on the deck to avoid being detected by the SAMs' Fan Song radar. We both had fully-up systems'.

As they went 'feet-dry' in a combat-spread formation, the crews began receiving MiG calls from *Red Crown*, but due to a radio problem, Cannon only picked some of these transmissions. Thus, he was aware that the section was on some sort of MiG vector, but he did not know the location of the MiGs.

About 30 nautical miles inland, the VF-51 crews saw a solid white parachute pass between them. They noted that the man hanging below the canopy was of small stature, and surmised that he was a VPAF pilot who had been shot down.

They had a brief glimpse of a possible MiG-21 at their 'three o'clock', but after a couple of check turns returned to their original degrees vector. About a minute later the Phantom IIs, now about 40 nautical miles inland, picked up a plan view of a MiG-17 at 1000 ft,

One of the last units to transition onto the Phantom II, VF-51 had a 'hardcore of ex-F-8H fighter jocks' within its ranks when it discarded its much-loved Crusaders for combat-weary F-4Bs in 1971. The eight 'gunfighters' that stayed on with the 'Screaming Eagles' following the conversion are seen together at NAS Miramar in the late spring of 1971. They are, from left to right (standing), Lt Ken Cannon, squadron XO Cdr 'Tooter' Teague, squadron CO Tom Tucker, Lt Dave Palmer and Lt Don Scott. And in the front row (left to right), Lt Rick Bradley, Lt Cdr Chuck Schroeder and Lt Cdr 'Devil' Houston. Cannon, Teague and Houston would all down MiGs the following year. The transition from the F-8 to the F-4 was not all plain sailing, as 'Devil' Houston remembers, 'We had been single-seat F-8 pilots, and as such we'd ridiculed all multi-crewed aircraft, especially the "Phantom phlyers". No we were becoming some of, well . . . *them*! Our hardcore philosophy going in was that there wasn't then, nor would there ever be, an NFO we'd rather have than an extra 500 lbs of fuel and the 20 mm cannons we were sacrificing by leaving the F-8s. Word of how we felt soon got about at Miramar, and it was with a great deal of reluctance that F-4 pilots and NFOs accepted orders to VF-51' (*Jerry Houston*)

just two nautical miles away in their '11 o'clock' position, heading due north at an estimated 350 knots.

The F-4s turned slightly left 'to put the MiG on their nose'. Apparently, the MiG pilot saw the Phantom IIs and started a right turn, slightly nose high, into them. 'He could have pulled that aircraft hard enough to meet us head-on', Cannon said of the MiG, 'but he didn't choose to do that'.

Cannon gave this description of the preliminary moves in the engagement. 'We were looking at him at about 90 degrees off, and Schroeder more or less became the engaged fighter. He started pulling his nose up and I pulled my nose higher and started climbing to a cover position on him. At this time, Schroeder looked like he was in good shape on him. He started to turn with him, and he had a tone after 45 degrees of turn. The engagement lasted through 270 degrees of turn, and I would say that the MiG probably climbed to 2000 ft.

'I was on the inside of the turn, topping out at about 7000 ft. I was sitting on my back, directly above the fight, trying to get separation on the guy. During the whole engagement I had a nice planform view of the top of the MiG-l7'.

Taking advantage of the Phantom II's superior speed, Schroeder closed on the MiG with a 150-knot overtake. After about 90 degrees of turn, the VPAF pilot performed a high-G, square-corner type barrel-roll-underneath manoeuvre, and ended up at Schroeder's 'six o'clock'. The VF-51 pilot called, 'Okay, he's at my "six". I'm extending 180 degrees'. However, the MiG was not a big threat at that point for he was not shooting, and was more than 3000 ft behind the lead F-4.

Once Schroeder started to extend and accelerate, the MiG pilot wasted no time in chasing him. He lit his afterburner for about two seconds and made a 180-degree, nose low left turn back in the direction of Hanoi. From his position overhead, Cannon saw the MiG's manoeuvre and called to Schroeder, 'He's breaking off, headed 360 degrees – bring it back to port'. Then Cannon rolled over the top and let his nose fall through. He repeated this call, but Schroeder still did not receive it, and continued to extend out of the fight. Cannon takes up the story;

'As soon as I got my nose on the MiG and put him in my gunsight, I got a beautiful tone. He was in a reversal from his hard port turn to a starboard turn. It looked like a slow-motion roll at that speed and altitude. He didn't have the control response to really whip it over, and

Coral Sea's commanding officer, Capt Bill Harris, got to congratulate his 'MiG killing' fighter crews no less than five times on the flightdeck of his carrier during the vessel's 1971-72 *WestPac*. This photograph was taken on the third of those occasions, on 10 May, when VF-51's Lt Ken Cannon (helmet off) and RIO Lt Roy Morris (extreme right) downed a MiG-17 20 miles south of Hanoi. This kill was the last of 11 MiGs destroyed by American fighters on 10 May 1972. Eight of these victories were credited to Navy F-4s (*Jerry Houston*)

that's where I caught him, right at his "dead six". I fired with 1G on the aircraft, and I doubt he had 2G on the MiG-17, because he was in this roll trying to reverse to starboard. I estimated the distance to be 3000 ft when I pulled the trigger.

'It seemed like an eternity before the missile came off the rail, but finally it powered away. It was a beautiful shot. The missile exploded right in his tail and parts of it started falling off. He began a slow roll back to port and slowly nosed over, impacting the ground in a near vertical dive. I had closed to 1500-1000 ft, and thought somebody was after me when I flew through all the debris coming down on both sides of the canopy.'

With the MiG now gone, the two F-4s rejoined and proceeded 'feet-wet'. Keeping down on the deck, Cannon jinked until he got back over the water, then rejoined Schroeder and headed for a tanker. Because of the heavy MiG activity, *Red Crown* had originally intended to refuel the Phantom IIs and return them to the area. However, the action quietened down just before they came off the tanker, so the VF-51 crews returned to their ship.

Cannon remembers, 'We seemed to have had problems hearing one another in MiG engagements. I think one of our big problems was the Sidewinder tone. We had discussed the possibility of having the tone in the front seat only so the RIOs could hear a little better'.

Again, experience played an important part in this victory, for according to Cannon (an ex-*Have Drill* pilot with personal experience of flying against a MiG-17 in the US), 'from what I saw, the MiG's manoeuvre was basically the same manoeuvre used against the F-4 and F-8 in *'Drill*. With one of our aircraft at his "six", the high-G, square-corner manoeuvre that he did was basically the same thing that I saw in *Have Drill*.

'I think the way *Have Drill* helped me the most was by simply exposing me to the MiG-17. You can sit around and talk at the bar all you want about the "square corner" the MiG-17 can turn, but until you've seen it with your own eyes, you can't visualise the way this thing can turn. It wasn't that big a surprise to me. I was expecting the MiG-17 to do that, and it looked the same as it did in *Have Drill*, where I initially saw it.'

Cannon added, 'Our training had a lot to do with our success, because the manoeuvres we flew all came more or less automatically to us. Nothing much was said, but we did end up in the classic fighter-cover, two-on-one situation. I fought using the same tactics that I had been taught during *Have Drill*, except for the fact that we were at a much lower altitude.'

'Bud' Morris voiced the following opinions in the wake of this engagement. 'From past experience, I was convinced there had to be another MiG-17 there. Therefore, I never stopped looking until we were feet-wet. I never did see another MiG, but I was looking. The only time I changed that aft lookout doctrine was when I saw the Sidewinder come off the rail, and I did it to see if the missile would hit. As far as the RIO goes, I can't stress enough how important it is for him to be looking outside being defensive while the pilot's being offensive'.

During the climactic air battles of 10 May, a total of 294 sorties were flown against North Vietnam by the Navy, with a further 120 by the Air Force. These aircraft were met by at least 39 VPAF MiGs – 14 MiG-17s, eight MiG-19s and 17 MiG-21s.

COLOUR PLATES

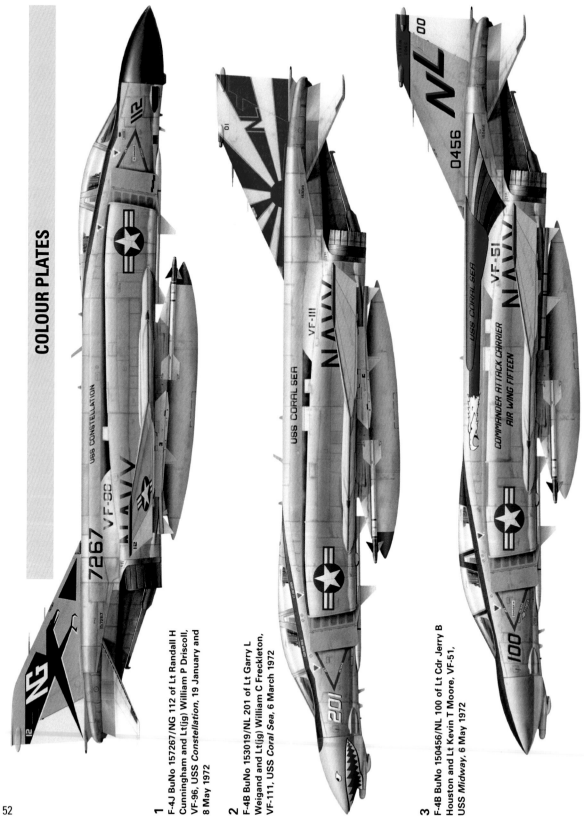

1
F-4J BuNo 157267/NG 112 of Lt Randall H
Cunningham and Lt(jg) William P Driscoll,
VF-96, USS *Constellation*, 19 January and
8 May 1972

2
F-4B BuNo 153019/NL 201 of Lt Garry L
Weigand and Lt(jg) William C Freckleton,
VF-111, USS *Coral Sea*, 6 March 1972

3
F-4B BuNo 150456/NL 100 of Lt Cdr Jerry B
Houston and Lt Kevin T Moore, VF-51,
USS *Midway*, 6 May 1972

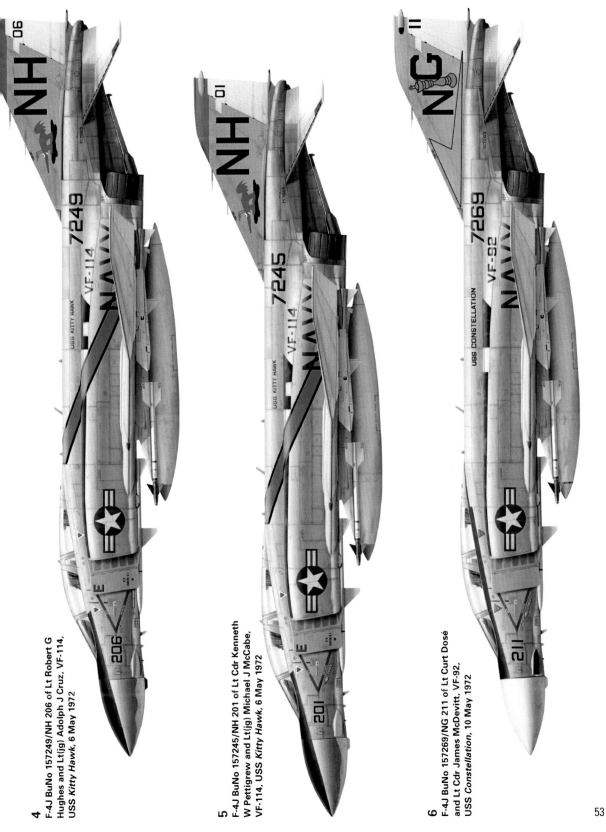

4
F-4J BuNo 157249/NH 206 of Lt Robert G
Hughes and Lt(jg) Adolph J Cruz, VF-114,
USS *Kitty Hawk*, 6 May 1972

5
F-4J BuNo 157245/NH 201 of Lt Cdr Kenneth
W Pettigrew and Lt(jg) Michael J McCabe,
VF-114, USS *Kitty Hawk*, 6 May 1972

6
F-4J BuNo 157269/NG 211 of Lt Curt Dosé
and Lt Cdr James McDevitt, VF-92,
USS *Constellation*, 10 May 1972

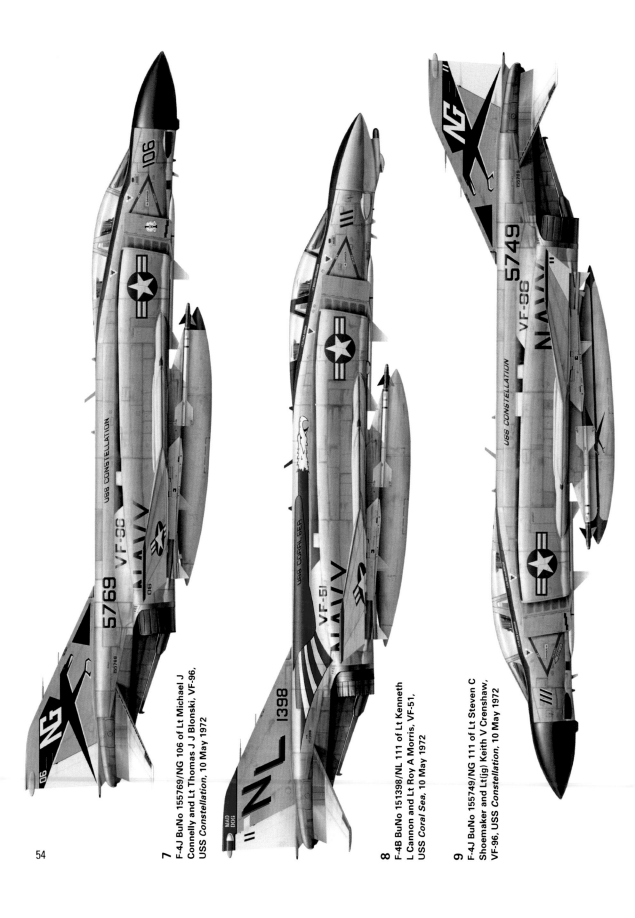

7
F-4J BuNo 155769/NG 106 of Lt Michael J
Connelly and Lt Thomas J J Blonski, VF-96,
USS *Constellation*, 10 May 1972

8
F-4B BuNo 151398/NL 111 of Lt Kenneth
L Cannon and Lt Roy A Morris, VF-51,
USS *Coral Sea*, 10 May 1972

9
F-4J BuNo 155749/NG 111 of Lt Steven C
Shoemaker and Lt(jg) Keith V Crenshaw,
VF-96, USS *Constellation*, 10 May 1972

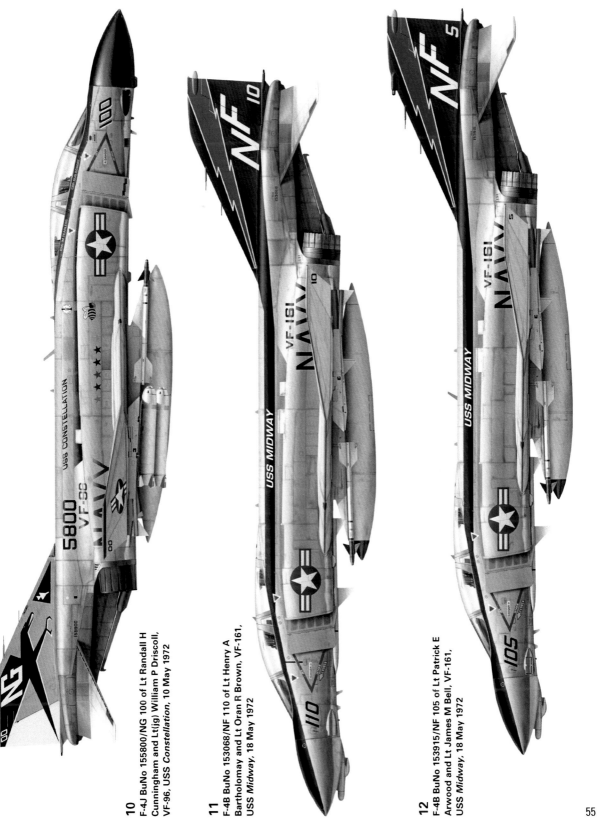

10
F-4J BuNo 155800/NG 100 of Lt Randall H
Cunningham and Lt(jg) William P Driscoll,
VF-96, USS *Constellation*, 10 May 1972

11
F-4B BuNo 153068/NF 110 of Lt Henry A
Bartholomay and Lt Oran R Brown, VF-161,
USS *Midway*, 18 May 1972

12
F-4B BuNo 153915/NF 105 of Lt Patrick E
Arwood and Lt James M Bell, VF-161,
USS *Midway*, 18 May 1972

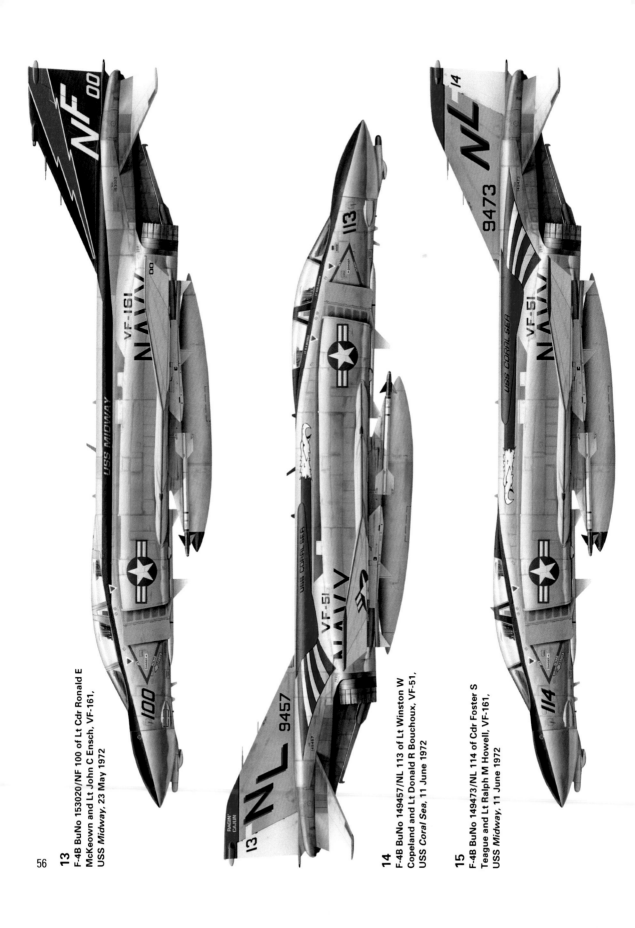

13
F-4B BuNo 153020/NF 100 of Lt Cdr Ronald E
McKeown and Lt John C Ensch, VF-161,
USS *Midway*, 23 May 1972

14
F-4B BuNo 149457/NL 113 of Lt Winston W
Copeland and Lt Donald R Bouchoux, VF-51,
USS *Coral Sea*, 11 June 1972

15
F-4B BuNo 149473/NL 114 of Cdr Foster S
Teague and Lt Ralph M Howell, VF-161,
USS *Midway*, 11 June 1972

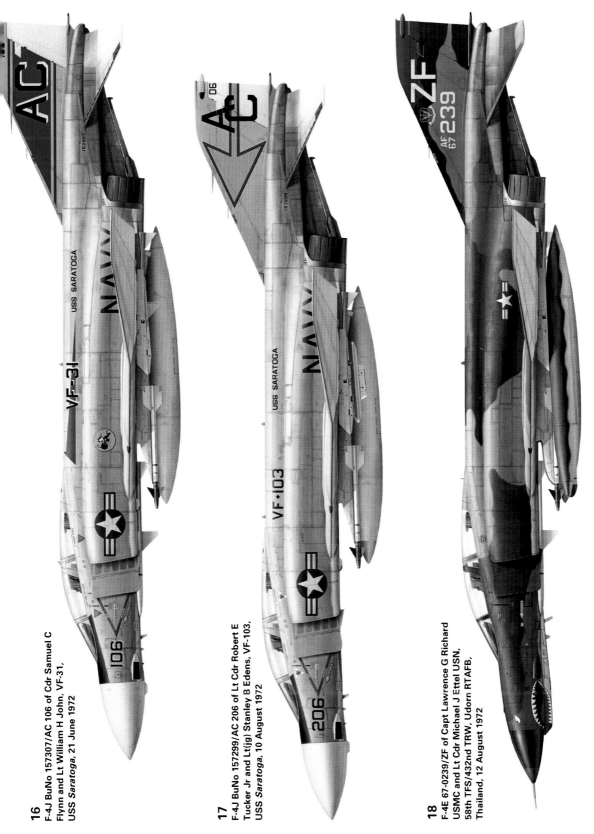

16
F-4J BuNo 157307/AC 106 of Cdr Samuel C
Flynn and Lt William H John, VF-31,
USS *Saratoga*, 21 June 1972

17
F-4J BuNo 157299/AC 206 of Lt Cdr Robert E
Tucker Jr and Lt(jg) Stanley B Edens, VF-103,
USS *Saratoga*, 10 August 1972

18
F-4E 67-0239/ZF of Capt Lawrence G Richard
USMC and Lt Cdr Michael J Ettel USN,
58th TFS/432nd TRW, Udorn RTAFB,
Thailand, 12 August 1972

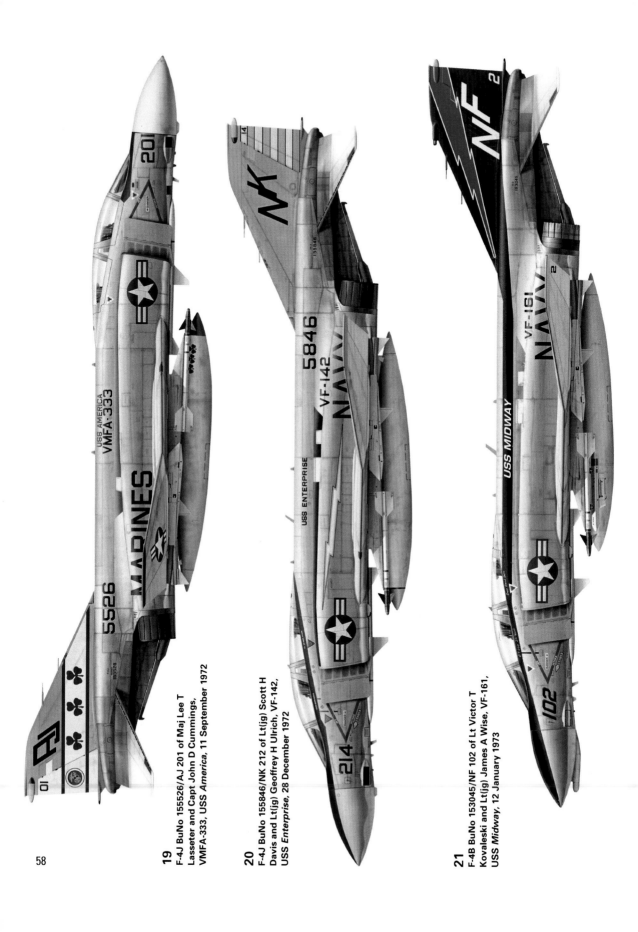

58

19
F-4J BuNo 155526/AJ 201 of Maj Lee T
Lasseter and Capt John D Cummings,
VMFA-333, USS *America*, 11 September 1972

20
F-4J BuNo 155846/NK 212 of Lt(jg) Scott H
Davis and Lt(jg) Geoffrey H Ulrich, VF-142,
USS *Enterprise*, 28 December 1972

21
F-4B BuNo 153045/NF 102 of Lt Victor T
Kovaleski and Lt(jg) James A Wise, VF-161,
USS *Midway*, 12 January 1973

1

2

3

4

5

6

7

8

9

10

11

12

13

14

15

16

17

18

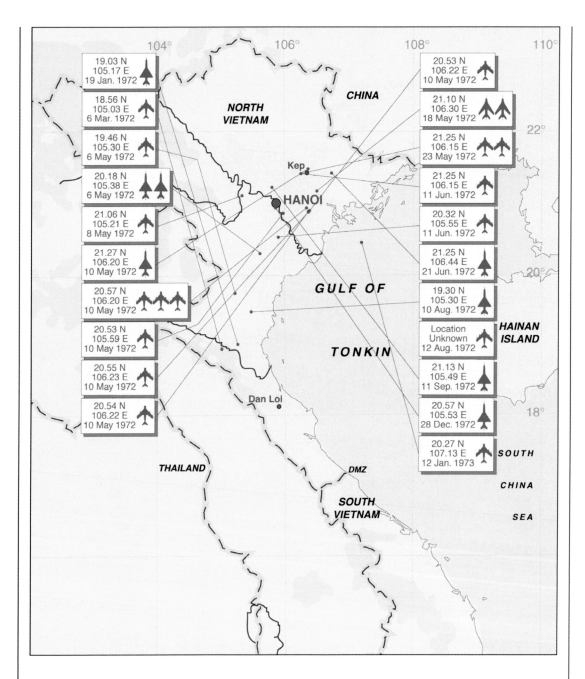

This map shows the approximate locations of all the *Linebacker* MiG kills recorded by Navy and Marine Corps crews flying from aircraft carriers or on exchange duty with the USAF. The vast majority of these victories were claimed around the Hanoi area

LINEBACKER I IN FULL EARNEST

Although the intensity of the aerial action of 10 May 1972 would never again be repeated, two more engagements later that month would result in a further four MiG kills for Navy F-4s.

Two of these victories occurred on 18 May during a large Alpha strike on the Haiphong highway and rail bridge. The MiGCAP support for the strike consisted of two F-4Bs from VF-161, embarked in USS *Midway* (CVA-41). These aircraft were crewed by Lts Henry A 'Bart' Bartholomay and Oran R Brown in the lead jet (BuNo 153068, call sign 'Rock River 110') and Lts Patrick E 'Pat' Arwood and James M 'Taco' Bell flying wing (in BuNo 153915, call sign 'Rock River 105'). The strike force was made up of eleven A-7Bs, four F-4Bs and three A-6As, all with mixed bomb loads, plus the normal supporting aircraft.

Following the launch from *Midway*, the two F-4Bs tanked off shore. The original plan called for the escorts to coast in north of Hon Gai, then follow a ridge of hills to their CAP station five miles south of Kep. This route offered radar cover from the ridge, and also put the jets in an area where few SAM sites were located. But Bartholomay experienced problems with his basket during tanking, and now the only way for them to arrive on-station on-time was to fly straight up the Red River, over Haiphong and then on to Kep.

When Bartholomay and Arwood finally reached their assigned CAP station, they were in combat-spread, with 'Rock River 105' on the right. During their ingress, RIO Bell busied himself studying the radar scope, looking for signs of a contact. But as soon as they received a 'bogey' call from *Red Crown*, Bell pulled his head out of the cockpit and started looking for MiGs outside.

As they continued their orbit, Bartholomay looked to his right to check his wingman and saw two sun-flashes low against a ridgeline at his 'two o'clock' position at an estimated range of 7-8 nautical miles. Recognising these flashes as potential 'bogies', he immediately called for a right turn, lit his afterburner and turned into Arwood. While crossing to Bartholomay's left side, Arwood also acquired a tally-ho. The section accelerated to about 650-675 knots and closed up.

In a rare example of inter-air wing operability, three F-4Bs from VF-161 drop their Mk 82s alongside a trio of A-7Cs from VA-86, assigned to CVW-8 aboard the *America*. The aircraft are conducting a Loran (Long range navigation) attack on a target 'up north', bombing through a moderate undercast (*via Angelo Romano*)

Bartholomay soon identified the two contacts as MiG-19s, then called that he was going to go 'shooter' and directed Arwood to go 'protective cover'. The MiGs (from the 925th Regiment) were just entering into the break on their approach to their airfield at Kep following a flight from China. The chase took the section directly to the VPAF base. Bartholomay begins his account;

'They appeared to see us about a mile west of Kep, as they started a port turn, still in trail. I was at 300 to 500 ft AGL (Above Ground Level), crossing the northern edge of the runway. The MiGs were level with me, and I told Arwood that I was going to push them around to port. Moments later I saw both their tanks come off simultaneously.'

The MiGs stayed in a level 3-4G turn for 360 degrees as Bartholomay maintained a lag-pursuit position about 1.5 nautical miles behind. Bartholomay continues;

'To let Arwood and Bell get out of phase with me and come in for a shot, I started a lag-pursuit at about 550 knots, pushing them around. Two or three times in the first 180 degrees of turn I tried to pull my nose up to them for a shot, but they recognised it and added another G or two and spoiled my solution.'

As the two F-4s completed the first 360-degree turn, the MiGs were close together in front of them. Arwood was about 3000 ft high, to the inside of the turn, with a good sight-picture of the lead MiG. Here, he describes what happened next;

'I had my pipper on him and was at a range of about 4500 ft, but I couldn't get a tone, so I kept trying. He was almost wings-level, with maybe a little right turn. I felt like I was almost "dead six". I was closing on him, so I fired the missile anyway.'

When the AIM-9 was fired, the lead MiG broke hard left as its wing continued right. Bartholomay commented, 'I felt that guy really laid on the G when Arwood shot his missile. He almost pulled the wings off'. The missile went ballistic and passed about 190 ft behind the MiG. Arwood estimated his speed at 400-450 knots, with about 50 knots of closure, at the time the missile was fired.

The MiGs immediately separated after Arwood fired his Sidewinder. Bartholomay followed the trailing MiG as it turned right, while Arwood

The crew of F-4B 'Rock River 105' (BuNo 153915) top off their tanks from a buddy store-equipped A-7B of VA-93 prior to heading into North Vietnam on a CAP mission. This aircraft downed a MiG-19 on 18 May 1972 whilst being flown by Lts 'Pat' Arwood and James 'Taco' Bell. Accepted at St Louis by the Navy on 30 November 1966, BuNo 153915 initially remained on site in Missouri with McDonnell undertaking research and development flights. On 10 March 1967 it was transferred to VF-121 at Miramar, and the fighter served with the unit until 13 July, when it was issued to VF-161. Completing two *WestPac/* Vietnam cruises with the 'Chargers' aboard the *Coral Sea* (7 September 1968 to 19 April 1969) and *Midway* (23 September 1969 to 1 July 1970), the jet then spent 16 months in NARF North Island being overhauled. Emerging from its lengthy maintenance period, BuNo 153915 returned to VF-161 and headed for the war zone, again on CVA-41, on 10 April 1972. Arriving back at Miramar on 3 March 1973, the F-4B switched coasts and joined Oceana-based VF-41 just 11 days after departing the *Midway*. BuNo 153915 was transferred to VMFAT-101 at Yuma prior to VF-41 deploying to the Mediterranean, and the jet served with the Marine training unit from 23 August 1973 through to 1 January 1975. Despatched to NARF North Island the following month, BuNo 153915 returned to fleet service with VF-111 in March 1976 as an F-4N. It remained (*continued on page 67*)

with the 'Sundowners' until the unit deployed on a Mediterranean cruise in October 1976, BuNo 153915 staying in California when it was sent to MCAS El Toro and VMFA-314. The jet flew with the Marines through to February 1982, when it returned to NAS North Island for overhaul. Back in fleet service eight months later, BuNo 153915 joined VF-154 at Miramar, and participated in the unit's final cruise with the Phantom II the following year. Deploying aboard the *Coral Sea* in March 1983, the 'Black Knights' completed a world cruise with the veteran carrier that lasted until 12 September. On 4 November the fighter participated in a flypast at Miramar which marked the retirement of the last US-based frontline Navy Phantom IIs. Sent to NARF Pensacola 13 days later, BuNo 153915 was administratively stricken (having amassed 4376 flight hours) within 24 hours and transferred to the Naval Aviation Museum at NAS Pensacola. It is presently displayed within this facility as VF-154's NK 101. When VF-161's double 'MiG killer' Jack 'Fingers' Ensch first saw the Phantom II displayed in the museum in 1991-92, he pointed out the jet's historical wartime significance to the museum curator, making a case that it should be repainted in the same VF-161 scheme that it wore when it got its MiG-19. 'I think my suggestion fell on deaf ears. I was told that the aircraft was painted in a VF-154 scheme because that was the last squadron it had been assigned to, and that it carried former *Blue Angel* CO Larry "Hoss" Pearson's name beneath the cockpit because he had also been CO of VF-154. When my suggestion was disregarded, I never brought the subject up with the museum again. If they didn't see the historical significance of the aircraft being a "MiG killer", I figured "the hell with them" – so much for historical accuracy! To me the historical significance of the aircraft being a "MiG killer" should have taken precedence over what squadron it was last assigned to, or who might have been that squadron's former CO' (*via Angelo Romano*)

pitched up into a nose high, left turn to follow the lead jet. Continuing his account of the engagement, Arwood said, 'The lead MiG was heading in a south-easterly direction, and I was high above him, coming down. As he continued his extension manoeuvre, he was rolling his aircraft from a 90-degree left to a 90-degree right bank. He was not really changing his flightpath any, but was rolling in an attempt to regain me visually'.

The lead MiG suddenly made a hard left turn, which caused Arwood to momentarily lose sight of it. He continued his left turn, however, and regained visual contact whilst still in a lag-pursuit position behind the MiG. The jet briefly continued its left turn, then pulled its nose up slightly and started reversing to the right. Arwood was now in a good tracking position behind the lead MiG, and he could see Bartholomay closing on the MiG ahead of him.

Just as the lead VPAF jet pulled its nose to the right, Arwood fired off his second Sidewinder. The missile tracked and exploded about five feet behind and to the right of the MiG. A split second later, Arwood saw part of the aircraft come off, followed by a bright flash in the tailpipe. The MiG then went out of control and the pilot ejected.

When the MiGs had split after Arwood fired his first missile, Bartholomay had gone to the belly side of the second MiG. Here, he recalls his opponent's reaction. 'He gave a "flip-flop" of his wings about three times and padlocked me at his "5.30" as I was pulling my nose up to him. As soon as he saw me, he pulled 6-7G and gave me a beautiful plan view, then extended'. Returning to lag-pursuit, Bartholomay made another attempt to pull his nose up to the second MiG, and was again met with a 7G turn.

Since his tactics were not working, Bartholomay unloaded and extended about two nautical miles to the west. He accelerated to 550 knots, picked up his nose about 20 degrees and pulled hard left into the MiG while it continued its left turn. Describing his actions, Bartholomay said, 'I lost sight of him (the second MiG) for about five to ten seconds, but my RIO still had him. He said, "Okay, he's at your 'nine o'clock' going to your '8.30'". So I said, "We're going to cause an overshoot here – call my turn". My RIO watched him go back to about "seven o'clock" and said, "Pull up now". I pulled up high into him and rolled to his outside and there he was, overshooting. It worked'.

Bartholomay continued his roll, but the second MiG countered by pulling up in front of him and rolling to the outside. 'As we both completed our rolls', Bartholomay recalled, 'I was looking at him at about "ten o'clock" some 1000 ft above me, both of us getting slow. I'd say he was at about 250 knots and I was doing about 220 knots, because he was still giving me nose-to-tail separation'.

While Bartholomay was in this slow-speed fight with the second MiG, the leader (who was being chased by Arwood and Bell) reached a position about two nautical miles behind 'Rock River 110'. Bartholomay then became concerned about his situation. Not wanting to slow down on his MiG while the lead MiG was closing at his 'five o'clock', he decided to unload. 'As it turned out, the (second) MiG had some hairy idea of dragging me out or trying to get away, because we simultaneously lowered our noses and started to extend.

'We went from about 220 knots to 400 knots, maintaining the same position and accelerating together. He was 1000-2000 ft in front of me

and I was in a lag-pursuit. My nose was behind him and I couldn't really pull it up'.

As they accelerated to about 400 knots, Bartholomay and Brown started gaining on the second MiG. 'I know he didn't see me back there', Bartholomay commented, 'for he started pulling up, and my RIO was calling the other MiG back about a mile-and-a-half, and closing. At this time Arwood shot his second missile and my RIO told me, "He got it – he got it". I said, "Great, we're in fat city". Just about ten seconds after that I pulled up and hosed my MiG with an AIM-9. It looked like the guy had gone into afterburner, and it apparently hit him in the tail because he spewed fuel or something. Then he pitched nose-up and went into a flat spiral'.

The entire engagement had taken place within three to five nautical miles of the runway at Kep airfield at altitudes between 150 and 6000 ft. No AAA activity was seen by Bartholomay and Arwood during the fight, even though the engagement lasted for a considerable time.

Both crews were surprised that they had not encountered any flak or SAMs during the engagement, or for that matter any other MiGs. Feeling somewhat lucky, the two joined up and headed 'feet wet' to tank, then back to the carrier. They were later told that two MiGs had given chase, and had come as close at ten miles before breaking off.

The *Red Baron* evaluators were critical of the engagement, noting that Bartholomay and Arwood had 'violated basic combat-spread principles when they separated for one-on-one attacks. The absence of other threats in the area allowed their split section to operate successfully'. Yet, this may well have been factored into the moment by the crews, who knew the situation in the air.

Like Cunningham before him, Bartholomay credited the success of his mission to the training he had received at Topgun, and the influence the school had had on overall fleet tactics. 'Our (VF-161) ACM training was a direct result of Topgun's influence on re-defining fighter tactics, and our squadron's insistence on spending more hours training its aircrews in these tactics than other squadrons did'.

A DOUBLE HAUL

Five days later, on 23 May, another crew from VF-161 tallied two more MiGs. This time, the Phantom IIs were part of a MiGCAP force supporting an Alpha strike sent to bomb a petroleum storage area to the north-east of Haiphong.

The strike force consisted of seven A-7Bs, three A-6As and five F-4Bs, carrying a mixed load of bombs, plus the normal supporting aircraft. Lead for the MiGCAP was flown by Lt Cdr Ronald E 'Mugs' McKeown and

From the left, Lts Oran Brown, 'Bart' Bartholomay, Pat Arwood and 'Taco' Bell celebrate downing the Navy's only MiG-19 kills of the Vietnam War. They had achieved their success during a late afternoon MiGCAP mission mounted near Kep airfield on 18 May 1972. In claiming a kill, Pat Arwood achieved the unique distinction of downing a MiG on his first mission over North Vietnam, as his RIO, 'Taco' Bell, explains. 'I was flying RIO with "nugget" (new guy) Pat Arwood. He had only about 150 hours of flying time in the F-4 when we arrived on *Yankee Station*. I had two previous combat cruises, but on each of them we had only worked in Laos and South Vietnam. During our first week on station, Pat and I only flew BARCAPs, and until the day we got our MiG, neither of us had flown over North Vietnam!'
(*via Peter Mersky*)

Lt John C 'Jack' Ensch (in BuNo 153020, call sign 'Rock River 100'), with Lt Mike Rabb and Lt(jg) Ken Crandall on their wing. Their assigned MiGCAP station was north of Hai Duong over the western edge of the ridge line approaching Kep, about 40 nautical miles from Hanoi.

McKeown and Rabb coasted in over Cam Pha (some 80 nautical miles from Hanoi), turned west and then headed down the karst ridges towards their CAP station, taking the same route flown by Bartholo-may and Arwood a few days earlier. Ingress was at 7000 ft at 480-500 knots.

When the MiGCAP package reached a position due north of Haiphong, *Red Crown* (operating that day from the guided missile frigate USS *Biddle* (DLG-34)) radioed a warning of bandits at 280 degrees and 35 nautical miles, then vectored the F-4s towards the contacts. But McKeown was having no success in establishing radar contact and Rabb's radar was inoperative, the latter having gone 'down' during the coast-in. Yet *Red Crown* continued updating the bandits' position with relative bearing calls.

When the two F-4s were about halfway between their initial vector point and Kep, *Red Crown* called, 'They're low, they're low'. McKeown and Rabb then descended to about 4000 ft to improve their radar search coverage.

As McKeown passed about two nautical miles north-east of the Kep runway, he called, 'I've got two "bogies" on the nose at about five miles'. Rabb then called a 'tally-ho'. Ensch immediately got a radar paint on the MiGs, but could not acquire radar lock due to ground clutter. McKeown added this account of the engagement. 'We were trying to lock them up to get some idea of closure. The next thing we knew they were on us, flying right between the section. The only thing we could do was cross-turn'.

As the two MiG-19s passed between them, the F-4s started a cross-turn, with McKeown going high. 'As we got high', McKeown remembers, 'I looked around and it was "raining"| MiG-17s on us. There were MiG-17s everywhere, and I think all of us thought that we were "up to our ass in alligators". Loose-deuce tactics from that point seemed to break down. There was no isolating any one MiG'.

As the section completed the first quarter of its cross-turn, four MiG-17s attacked from about 1000 ft, and Rabb was immediately engaged. He recalled, 'The two that turned on me (the second section of MiG-17s) had already achieved a high deflection-type shot following an almost 90-degree turn. It seemed like they were on a pedestal turning through the sky. I initiated a break-turn into the closest MiG-17 and he rendezvoused on me. I'd say within the next 270 degress of the turn he achieved a really fine firing position. He was not much more than 500 ft away, pulling lead and firing.

Still wearing their sweat-soaked flightsuits, Jack Ensch (left) and 'Mugs' McKeown (centre) give a light-hearted debriefing of their double 'MiG-killing' mission in the VF-161 ready room soon after returning to CVA-41 on 23 May 1972. CVW-5 CAG, Cdr 'CE' Myers, looks on with amusement (*via Angelo Romano*)

'I remember having it run through my mind whether or not I should continue the hard-as-possible break into this guy or attempt the roll-away manoeuvre. My instinct was to keep turning into him'.

Rabb then entered a 7G, nose-low spiral and descended to about 50 ft. During the spiral, the MiG-17 slid slightly outside and high on Rabb. Meanwhile, McKeown had come around into the fight after his cross-turn. 'I had expected them to fight horizontally', he said, 'but they weren't. They were fighting mostly in the vertical'.

Seeing a MiG-19 low, McKeown started pulling for it. 'As I was pulling', he continued, 'I looked up and saw the belly of a MiG-17 coming right down at us, head-on. I thought, "Oh, Jesus, we're going to have a mid-air". We missed him by about 25 ft'.

As soon as the MiG-17 passed, McKeown pulled back into it as hard as he could. 'We were in a hard, nose-high turn, 30 degrees nose up, pulling around hard to the right in heavy buffet. It was classic for the F-4. The stick started lightening on me, I kept pulling, and then the jet went out of control. It rolled back left over the top about two rolls. As soon as I got over on my back, I pushed full forward-stick. The F-4 completed about one-and-a-half more rolls and came out inverted.

'I got it into to my head that we were going to spend the night in this little valley, eat pumpkin soup and have our name on a bracelet. All these things flashed through my mind, but as soon as the F-4 popped out at 1800 to 2000 ft, it was "right back into the fight and kill somebody".'

When McKeown recovered from his departure, he looked up and saw a MiG-17 in front of him. He pulled in behind the VPAF jet, got a good tone and fired an AIM-9G. 'All of a sudden he really cranked it around', McKeown remembers, 'and the target went from being a "dead six" to about a 90-degree shot, just like that. He was in 'burner, and the missile seemed to guide by him. It went right by his tail'.

By now McKeown had seen Rabb and Crandall with a MiG-17 directly behind them, firing its deadly 37 mm cannon shells in their direction.

Photographed by an RF-8G photo-recce pilot from CVW-5's VFP-63 Det 3, two clean F-4Bs from VF-161 cruise at altitude over the Pacific soon after embarking on the *Midway* at the start of the unit's sixth, and last, wartime *WestPac*. This deployment would last for 205 days, and see VF-161 fly 2322 sorties. Led by Cdr Wayne 'Deacon' Connell (his assigned jet – BuNo 152243 – is seen in the foreground of this photo), who placed great emphasis on ACM training for his crews, VF-161 would enjoy unparalleled success on this cruise, downing five MiGs and winning the Adm Joseph Clifton award as the best fighter squadron in the Navy (*Mike Rabb via Jack Ensch*)

'Extend and take him out', McKeown called, as he manoeuvred behind the MiG. Firing a single Sidewinder (which missed), McKeown continued to pursue the enemy jet across the circle as it worked its way down to about 200 ft. When the MiG picked up its nose and started to climb, he got a good tone and loosed off another missile, which tracked directly to the MiG. The missile tore pieces of the jet's tail and the VPAF fighter flipped over on its back and went down.

As McKeown started to leave, Ensch called, 'We've got one at "4.30", and he's gunning'. They could see the MiG's belly, and the 37 mm cannon rounds were passing in front of them. McKeown continues, 'He was pulling lead on us and working. I'd heard reports that guys broke into a MiG forcing the overshoot. We had pretty good airspeed – about 400+ knots – so we tried it and made a hard turn into him. I broke really hard into him and hell, he had read the report! He dug inside our turn and started rendezvousing on us. All of a sudden it hit me. I shouted, "He can't see me! The bastard can't see me!"'

Because the MiG pilot was pulling such a large amount of lead, McKeown knew his Phantom II was in his opponent's blind spot. He went on to say;

'As soon as it hit me that he couldn't see us, I pushed negative-G, unloaded, came out of 'burner and watched him turn inside of us. He flew right by the starboard side. When we didn't fly out in front of him, he broke back to the left with that really slow roll rate synonymous with the MiG-17. He was nose high, and we just rolled in behind him. I got behind him, had a good tone, fired a Sidewinder and that one went right up the tailpipe. It blew up and the guy ejected.'

Immediately after McKeown and Ensch's second kill, the two Phantom IIs joined in combat-spread and exited the area without further incident.

McKeown estimated that all of his AIM-9G firings were at a range of 3000 ft or less, looking right up the tailpipe of the MiG with very little track-crossing angle.

McKeown and Rabb's flying was outstanding that day, especially considering the four-to-one odds each crew faced. In early August McKeown received orders to report to Topgun to take over as CO of the Navy Fighter Weapons School. Jack Ensch, however, remained with the 'Chargers' aboard *Midway*, and he was shot down (in their MiG killing jet, BuNo 153020) on 25 August by a SAM, becoming a PoW for the war's duration. Ensch was badly injured in this action, and his pilot, Lt Cdr Michael Doyle, failed to survive the shootdown.

As May came to an end, the Navy's F-4 force tallied 16 MiGs (eleven MiG-17s, two MiG-19s

A highly experienced two-tour combat veteran by the time he 'bagged' his two MiG-17s on 23 May 1972, Lt Jack Ensch is seen climbing aboard a 'Chargers' F-4B on the *Midway* in mid-1972 (*Jack Ensch*)

On 25 August 1972, Jack Ensch and his pilot Lt Cdr Mike Doyle were shot down by a SAM. Ensch was badly injured in the high speed ejection that followed, but survived as a PoW. Doyle was killed. On 29 March 1973 Ensch was returned to US authorities at Hanoi's Gia Lam airport, where this photo was taken. He was amongst the last group of PoWs to be released (*Jack Ensch*)

and three MiG-21s), and had endured the most serious aerial fighting of the war. And while the Navy had officially suffered no losses in air-to-air combat, an F-4 from VF-92 had been downed by AAA and a VF-96 jet destroyed by a SAM – both on 10 May.

THE RAIDS CONTINUE

Early June 1972 saw a downturn in activity from the previous month due in part to President Nixon's visit to Moscow. Indeed, from 25 May through 5 June, bombing was forbidden within a ten-mile radius of Hanoi as a political gesture towards the Soviets while Nixon prepared to discuss the Strategic Arms Limitations (SALT) Agreements with Premier Leonid Brezhnev. It was not long, however, before the Navy Phantom II crews were repeating their successes of the previous month.

On 11 June, two F-4Bs from VF-51 were part of a MiGCAP force from the *Coral Sea* supporting an Alpha strike of 14 A-7s, five F-4s and three A-6s on the Nam Dinh Thermal Plant and army barracks. Cdr Foster S 'Tooter' Teague and his RIO, Lt Ralph M Howell, crewed F-4B 'Screaming Eagle 114' (BuNo 149473), while Lts Winston W 'Mad Dog' Copeland and Donald R Bouchoux manned 'Screaming Eagle 113' (BuNo 149457) as their wing.

Teague, an ex-F-8 pilot, was Commanding Officer of VF-51, and he was regarded by all who knew him as a 'colourful' character! Copeland, a Topgun graduate, had been 'in hack' (restricted to his stateroom for an infraction), and had to be given special permission to fly this sortie.

'It seemed as if I lived in hack while in that squadron – three times in 18 months!' Copeland remembered years later. 'I was in hack on 11 June 1972 because a few days earlier I had flown a Phantom II from the boat to NAS Cubi Point, in the Philippines, to swap it out with another aeroplane on the beach. The RIO who flew with me went home on emergency leave, and I had to bring the replacement jet out to the ship two days later. I couldn't find a RIO on base, so I flew from Cubi Point back to the *Coral Sea*, on *Yankee Station*, single-seat (without a RIO), and by myself (a single aircraft versus a section, with a wingman).

'I calculated the charlie time (pre-planned landing on time) and caught a three-wire. As I was passing out mail in the ready room, the captain of the boat called "Tooter" Teague and asked him why I had landed single-seat on his boat! "Tooter" went a little crazy and sent me to my stateroom. No sense of humour! As a result, I lost my section leader qualification, and I could only fly with "Tooter", "Blackjack" (squadron XO Cdr Jack Finley), "Devil" (Lt Cdr Jack Houston) and Chuck Schroeder – thus I got to fly the best hops!'

Prior to the MiG-killing mission, Copeland and Bouchoux had not flown together before – Copeland's normal RIO, Lt(jg) Dale Arends, had flown the previous night and was exhausted. 'Mad Dog' had already made one Vietnam cruise with VF-151 aboard *Midway*, and had been transferred to VF-51 when it transitioned from Crusaders to Phantom IIs in mid-1970 to help with the evolution of squadron tactics against the MiGs

The two F-4Bs crossed the beach into North Vietnam at about 5000 ft, and 420 knots, and proceeded to their assigned MiGCAP station approximately 190 degrees and 25 nautical miles from *Bullseye*. Once on CAP, the two established a combat spread figure eight weave orbit at 3000 ft.

The Phantom IIs had been on station for about five or six minutes when *Red Crown* called, 'Bandits, 049 degrees at eight nautical miles'. Neither crew heard the controller due to radio difficulties, but the message was relayed by a nearby A-6.

Teague and Copeland had been on vector for about 90 seconds when Howell called 'tally ho' on four MiG-17s. The MiGs were at 800 ft in a 20- to 30-degree left bank, some 2.5 nautical miles off in their 'one-o'clock' position. The first section was about 500 ft apart in a loose fighting-wing formation. The trailing MiGs (numbers three and four) were separated by about 2000 ft to the right. Copeland then moved to the right of Teague and acquired a visual at his 'eleven o'clock'.

According to Teague, the MiGs did not yet see the VF-51 jets. 'I'm sure they didn't see us, and were looking up for us. We started an easy left turn into them. At about that time I think they saw us, because the formation started disintegrating'. Teague and Howell then started after the third MiG. 'The number one and number two MiGs came hard left, and the number three MiG went straight ahead, with the number four in a sort of gentle right turn. The number two MiG reversed right over the top of my canopy, and I told my RIO (Howell), "Watch that guy – he's going to our six". Teague continued, 'About that time he exploded right over the top of us!'

Copeland and Bouchoux had already pulled up to a cover position following their tally-ho. The pilot of 'Screaming Eagle 113' remembers, 'I pulled up and to the left a little bit, waiting for the leader of the first section to present his "six" to me for a belly shot. At that time he (MiG 2) saw Teague and Howell and began to roll over him. I was looking at the MiG about ten degrees off, 200 ft high, and approximately 2000 to 3000 ft in trail. I was closing at about 100 knots, so I tried to get my shot off as soon as I could. I knew I was going to be at minimum range shortly.

'I fired my Sidewinder and it seemed to take a week to get off the rails. It really only took about eight-tenths of a second, but time stood still. The missile went abruptly to the right, then immediately cut back towards the MiG. At first I thought it was going to miss, but it struck the MiG at the wing root and caused an immediate fireball. I had to pull up to miss it'. The MiG-17 then fell away in flames and hit the ground at high speed.

Copeland's evasive move put him and Bouchoux at a height of about 1000 ft, from where he saw the two remaining MiGs about 3000 ft in front of him 'in a fairly tight section formation'. But Copeland had now lost sight of Teague. He immediately scanned the skies and sighted his leader about 2000 ft off in his 'five o'clock' position. Copeland then tried to re-acquire the two fleeing MiGs, but they had quickly disappeared into a scattered cloud layer.

Capt Bill Harris 'pressed the flesh' with 'MiG killers' from VF-51 for the last time on 11 June 1972 after the 'Screaming Eagles' downed their final two victories of the war. Amused by their captain's congratulatory comments are, from left to right, VF-51 CO Cdr 'Tooter' Teague and Lts Ralph Howell, 'Mad Dog' Copeland and Don Bouchoux (*US Navy*)

VF-51's entire flying staff for its 1971-72 *WestPac* deployment pose on and in front of their CAG jet (BuNo 150456) aboard the *Coral Sea* soon after departing Alameda, California, on 12 November 1971. This was the aircraft that 'Devil' Houston (sat on the windscreen) and Kevin Moore used to down their MiG-17 on 6 May 1972. Delivered to the Navy from St Louis on 6 December 1962, it completed two combat deployments to Vietnam, seeing action with VF-161 from the *Coral Sea* between 26 July 1967 and 6 April 1968, and with VF-51 between 12 November 1971 and 17 July 1972. BuNo 150456 returned to the Gulf of Tonkin in 1973, again with VF-51 and CVA-43, and flew bombing missions over Cambodia. Upgraded into an F-4N, the fighter's next operational deployment was with VF-41 to the Mediterranean aboard USS *Franklin D Roosevelt* (CVA-42) in 1975. Transferred back to Miramar in July 1976 for service with reserve-manned VF-301, BuNo 150456 had flown with this unit for only a matter of months when it was sent to NARF North Island for overhaul. It next joined the Marine Corps reserve unit VMFA-321 at NAF Andrews, in Maryland, on 11 April 1977. Replaced by an F-4S in November 1984, the jet was duly sent to NARF Cherry Point, where it was converted into a QF-4N target drone. Issued to the Naval Weapons Center at China Lake, in California, in February 1986, BuNo 150456 was finally expended as a missile target on 27 January 1989. By then the fighter had accrued an impressive 5600 flying hours (*J Houston*)

Although Copeland missed Teague's encounter, Teague described it as follows from the point where he saw the explosion of MiG 2;

'The MiG that I was after (MiG 3) was still in a very gentle right turn, maybe 5-10 degrees angle-of-bank, but not pulling. We went through a little puffball cloud and I lost sight of him temporarily. When we came out, he was still in the gunsight. I could not get a tone on my first missile (an AIM-9). I could either go back in the cockpit and re-select another missile or fire that one off, hoping that I just had a bad tone system. I fired and it went ballistic. I immediately got a good tone on the next one and squeezed the second missile off. The second one went right up his tailpipe. He exploded and tumbled out of the sky.'

Teague then pressed his attack on MiG 4, which was still to the right at his 'one o'clock'. Teague and Howell turned, got a good tone, then launched their third AIM-9. Teague reported, 'About the time I squeezed the trigger, MiG 4 started into a hard, right turn with the missile in flight. He broke right, as only a MiG-17 can at about 350 knots, and the missile went ballistic. He went down our right side and had already completed about 90 degrees more turn than I had. We ended up at my wingman's deep "seven o'clock", streaking south with no MiGs in sight'.

It was at this point that the two MiGs reported by Copeland flew under the F-4Bs, heading north. Because the two Phantom IIs were experiencing radio problems, Teague was not able to call Copeland, and the MiGs disappeared.

As the two F-4Bs rejoined, the crews made a quick sweep of the area, seeing no MiGs. However, according to Copeland *Red Crown* reported that two MiG-21s had been vectored into their area, and the two Navy crews decided to 'bug out'. Both F-4s egressed a low altitude (about 50 ft above minimum level, and at nearly 550 knots), trying to avoid SAMs and the approaching MiGs. Copeland described this effort;

'We were jinking pretty hard – as much as we could without bleeding off too much airspeed. Seven miles from crossing "feet-wet", we had a port engine fire light illuminate in the cockpit. We hadn't felt any hits.'

Copeland said that he brought the port engine to idle, but the light refused to go out and the aeroplane continued to stream smoke. 'We debated briefly whether we should eject, but we were not real keen on spending time in Hanoi. So we decided to test our luck. As soon as we crossed "feet wet" I started a gentle climb at about 350 knots, shut down the left engine and took the right engine out of afterburner because I didn't want to be in 'burner with that fire back there. "Tooter" came over and told us that we had a fire around our left engine'.

When he reached the carrier, Copeland was waved off on his approach because the fire had apparently started again. The carrier then told the pilot to hold until the remaining strike aircraft had recovered. As Copeland and

Bouchoux climbed, the fire finally went out. However, they continued to trail smoke, and the two argued with the 'boat' as to whether to eject. Copeland finally won the day, making a single-engine landing. It was later discovered that their F-4B had taken two small-arms rounds just outboard of the left auxiliary-air door, which had severed fuel lines and an oil line, causing fuel to seep into the hot section of the left engine.

Winston Copeland went on to become an instructor at *Topgun*, and later continued his flying career as a CAG of CVW-1 (in 1986-88) and then captain of USS *America* (CV-66). He eventually reached the rank of rear admiral, and commanded the USS *Theodore Roosevelt* (CVN-71) Battle Group during Operation *Allied Force* over Kosovo and the former Yugoslavia in 1999.

ONE F-4 DOWN AND ONE MiG KILL

On 18 June, F-4J BuNo 157273 of VF-213, embarked in the *Kitty Hawk*, was lost when it was struck by 23 mm AAA whilst overflying Hon Nieu island. Its crew, Lt Cdr Roy Cash (a 'MiG killer' with VF-33 on 10 July 1968) and Lt R J Laib, were flying a BARCAP mission in support of a dawn attack on a merchant ship at the time. The jet was struck in the port wing and a fire erupted. Cash managed to fly the aircraft some 100 miles back towards his carrier before he and Laib were finally forced to eject. Both men were quickly picked up by a Navy helicopter.

Three days later VF-31 avenged this loss when squadron XO Cdr Sam Flynn and Lt(jg) Bill John 'bagged' a MiG-21. They were flying MiGCAP for a 21-aeroplane Alpha strike against the Co Gian SAM assembly area, the Doan Lai storage area and the Hai Dong marshalling yard at approximately 1215 hrs. Their F-4J (BuNo 157307, call sign 'Band Wagon 106') was armed with four AIM-9G Sidewinders and four AIM-7E-2 Sparrows, plus a 600-gallon centreline tank.

While maintaining their station, the section received a call from *Red Crown* that there were 'Blue Bandits,

Its glory days over, 'Screaming Eagle 113' sits in a forgotten corner of the NARF North Island facility in the mid-1970s, its once immaculate paint scheme now faded and streaked. As the MiG-17 silhouette on its splitter plate denotes, this machine was used by 'Mad Dog' Copeland and Don Bouchoux to claim VF-51's final kill of the Vietnam war on 11 June 1972. One of the oldest F-4s to see action in the *Linebacker* campaign, BuNo 149457 had been delivered to the Navy as an F4H-1 on 11 June 1962. A veteran of three combat cruises and a spell in-theatre with the Marines, it was retired by VF-51 in September 1973. Currently stored by the Naval Aviation Museum in Pensacola, BuNo 149457 had been displayed in front of the nearby Naval Aviation Schools Command for many years (*via Angelo Romano*)

VF-31's future 'MiG-killing' F-4J (BuNo 157307) heads north-east on a bombing mission with A-6As from VA-75 in mid-1972 (*via P Mersky*)

Tucked up beneath the wing of their leader, the crew of 'Bandwagon 106' (BuNo 157307) keep a watchful eye on the photographer as they head for the *Saratoga* at the end of yet another uneventful BARCAP in the autumn of 1972. Accepted by the Navy at St Louis on 18 December 1970, this F-4J served with VF-31 until September 1975, during which time it completed three Mediterranean cruises and a Vietnam deployment. Transferred to VF-33 six months later, it visited the Mediterranean with the unit aboard USS *Independence* (CV-62) from October 1975 to April 1976, and then moved to VF-74 in May 1977. BuNo 157307 undertook its fifth Med deployment (aboard the *Forrestal*) between April and October 1978. In September of the following year it moved once again, joining VF-103 and heading for the Mediterranean aboard the *Saratoga* in March 1980. BuNo 157307 joined fleet replacement squadron VF-171 at Oceana in October 1981, and stayed with this unit until sent to NARF North Island in April 1983 for upgrading to F-4S specification. The jet returned to service on 27 December 1983 when it was posted to VMFAT-101 at Yuma. Transferred to VMFA-232 at Kaneohe Bay in May 1987, the fighter was replaced by an F/A-18A in November 1988. BuNo 157307 was duly flown to Dulles International Airport, in Washington DC, on 29 November and transferred to the National Air and Space Museum, Smithsonian Institution, for eventual restoration and display (*via Peter Mersky*)

030 degrees at 17 nautical miles'. The two F-4 pilots immediately steered onto their new heading and accelerated to 400 knots at 11,000 ft. Flynn's wing, Lt(jg) Nick Strelcheck and Lt Dave Arnold, sighted the MiG-21s first, high in their 'one-o'clock' position at a range of four nautical miles. The MiGs were in a line-of-bearing formation, with the second MiG in trail about 40 degrees from the lead jet.

Neither MiG apparently saw the Phantom IIs at first. However, as soon as the two F-4s turned into them, the MiGs separated, with the lead bandit going high and the trailing MiG going low. Flynn then called tally-ho, and indicated that he was taking the high MiG. Strelcheck manoeuvred to provide cover. According to the *Red Baron* report, the engagement proceeded like this;

'MiG 1 went into a high yo-yo manoeuvre, followed by what looked like a rudder reversal into a steep nose-down 180-degree turn. In this manoeuvre, John attained a full-system radar lock-on. Flynn attempted to fire an AIM-7 at a range of two-and-a-quarter nautical miles. However, no missile came off the aircraft. Flynn looked into his aircraft and checked his switches. Noting that the aim-dot was just outside the ASE (Allowable Steering Error) circle, he squeezed again, but still could not get an AIM-7 to launch. By this time the lead MiG was starting to meet him head on, so he pulled up high, rolled onto his back, and pulled back towards the MiG.'

Cdr Flynn continues the description of the action;

'I saw him get his nose down – really steep down – and I was going to try the old "roll in at six" trick. I left my nose up and went into 90 degrees of bank and came down on him. I switched to "heat" and got a tone on him, looking down. When he saw me there, he levelled his wings and hauled ass right into the clouds, heading south. I actually got a growl on him but couldn't track long enough to get a Sidewinder off. He started opening on me right after I got the tone, and gave me an opening velocity of 100 knots or better. Then John came up and said, "There's one on 02's rear".'

The second MiG, which had separated low, had rejoined the fight and was now camped at about 3000 ft behind Flynn's wingman. The XO hollered at Strelcheck to 'keep turning', just as the MiG fired an Atoll missile. Flynn said, 'I knew it wasn't guiding and I didn't really sweat it. The Atoll went a good 1000 ft behind Strelcheck. I think that's when he unloaded, because I saw him start opening, and I breathed a sigh of relief.

Flynn had expected the MiG to start pulling its nose forward on his wing for a guns pass, but instead it continued in a lag-pursuit course. As Strelcheck began to accelerate away from the MiG-21, the bandit 'yo-yoed' off, giving Flynn the opportunity he needed for the kill.

Flynn obtained a good tone, then triggered an AIM-9 from about two miles. He commented, 'I wasn't

very happy with the range of the first Sidewinder. After that first shot, he bent it into me so hard that I was 90 degrees off. For some reason or other he eased off his turn, and when he did, I got a good growl. I shot the second Sidewinder and I told John, "We got him this time'". But Flynn's missile passed just aft of the MiG and 'apparently did not fuse'.

Flynn pulled his nose back onto the MiG and loosed off his third Sidewinder. This one, however, found its target. 'It didn't even matter if it fused or not', Flynn said, 'because it went right up his tailpipe'. The MiG went into a flat spin and the pilot ejected at about 2000 ft. Although a third MiG-21 circled above Flynn's section, it chose not to join the engagement. The XO called, 'Let's get out of here – keep your "six" clear', as the two Phantom IIs joined in a combat spread and exited the MiGCAP area.

Following this engagement, the *Red Baron* report noted that Flynn had benefited considerably from having flown the MiG-21J simulator at NASA. Commenting on this, the XO stated, 'I flew the NASA-operated MiG-21J simulator, where I learned that they (MiG pilots) were not flying the aeroplane on the ragged edge of the envelope. Instead, they were flying the aeroplane the way a relatively raw nugget or a returnee from a desk job would fly it'. *Red Baron* concluded that this training 'greatly enhanced Flynn's ability to effectively engage the MiG-21'.

The Navy's three MiGs in June raised its total to 21 VPAF aircraft in 1972 for the loss of just one F-4 in air-to-air combat. Given the successes of the Navy aircrews against MiGs, the VPAF refused to tackle Navy F-4s unless they had a distinct advantage. Indeed, following these June MiG engagements, the Navy would down only two more MiGs through to the end of *Linebacker I* in October, while losing two F-4s to MiGs.

As XO of VF-31, 'MiG killer' Cdr Sam Flynn had his victory silhouette applied to the splitter plate of his assigned aircraft, 'Bandwagon 102' (BuNo 157293). This in turn has led aviation historians to erroneously state that he was flying this machine when he claimed his MiG-21 on 21 June 1972 *(via P Mersky)*

Cdr Flynn applies the finishing touches to a MiG-21 kill marking on BuNo 157307, watched by his RIO, Lt(jg) Bill John *(via P Mersky)*

LINEBACKER I COMES TO AN END

Mid-summer saw a dramatic change in the North Vietnamese air defences. In April and May, American air forces had encountered significant MiG activity and heavy AAA and SAM fire. US losses from MiGs during that period totalled 24 aircraft (for all three services), plus many others from AAA and SAMs. Now, North Vietnamese air defences were severely damaged and depleted, the communists having expended much of their ordnance in the early days of *Linebacker I*.

Moreover, because the Americans had mined the North Vietnamese ports and heavily bombed the railways running from China to Hanoi, the North Vietnamese were unable to import Soviet or Chinese weaponry and ammunition, and thus were without replacements.

Despite these shortages, on 10 July the Navy lost another Phantom II to VPAF MiGs when a CAP flight of F-4Js from VF-103, embarked in USS *Saratoga* (CV-60), was engaged by several MiG-17s from the 923rd Fighter Regiment over Kep. BuNo 155803 (call sign 'Clubleaf 212'), crewed by Lts Robert Randall and Frederick Masterson, was hit by cannon fire whilst dogfighting with a MiG flown by Hanh Vinh Tuong. The aircraft caught fire and the crew ejected – both men were quickly captured. Minutes later Tuong himself was killed by an air-to-air missile, although official US records fail to list any claims for this date.

USS *Saratoga* (CV-60), embarking CVW-3, was hastily sent to the Gulf of Tonkin in April 1972 when the *Linebacker* campaign moved into top gear. An east coast carrier more used to patrolling the waters of the Mediterranean, 'Sara' performed just one combat cruise with Task Force 77. The vessel arrived on *Yankee Station* on 18 May 1972, and completed its seventh, and last, spell on the line on 8 January 1973. In that time its two Phantom II units had claimed two MiG-21s destroyed, but CVW-3 had in turn lost seven aircraft to AAA, five to SAMs and one to a MiG-17. A further four machines were lost in operational accidents (*via Peter Mersky*)

VF-103's CAG jet during its 1972-73 combat cruise on the *Saratoga* was F-4J BuNo 155826. CVW-3 was commanded at the time by Cdr Richard 'Deke' Bordone, who 'Sluggers' 'MiG killer' Lt Cdr Gene Tucker described as being 'one of naval aviation's top tacticians of that time' (*via Brad Elward*)

Included within this six-ship formation of VF-103 jets, all with their tailhooks extended, is 'MiG killer' 'Clubleaf 206' (BuNo 157299), which downed a MiG-21 on 10 August 1972, 'Clubleaf 212' (BuNo 155803), which was shot down by a MiG-17 on 10 July 1972, and 'Clubleaf 202' (BuNo 157302), which fell victim to AAA on 8 September 1972. The crew of 'Clubleaf 212' (Lts Robert Randall and Frederick Masterson) both ejected and were captured, and the crew of 'Clubleaf 202' (CAG Cdr 'Deke' Bordone and Lt J H Findley) 'banged out' in the vicinity of CV-60 and were quickly rescued. 'MiG killer' BuNo 157299 was handed over to the Navy at St Louis on 24 November 1970 and issued to VF-103 exactly one week later. The fighter would remain with the 'Sluggers' until February 1976, and in that time it would complete a series of Mediterranean deployments with CVW-3 aboard the *Saratoga*. The highlight of this period was the unit's sole foray to Vietnam in 1972-73. Sent to NARF Cherry Point in February 1976, the fighter remained in maintenance until 25 June, when it was issued to VF-11. BuNo 157299 was still serving with the 'Red Rippers' when it was lost in a flying accident on 9 February 1977. Participating in a daytime ACM training sortie from Oceana, the aircraft suffered an in-flight fire within the fuselage. After the pilot had descended to 9000 ft in an attempt to make it back to base, the aircraft went into an uncontrollable left roll and the crew were forced to eject (safely) while the jet was flying at 240 knots, and its left wing was 60 degrees down (*via Peter E Davies*)

VF-103 had to wait until 10 August to avenge this loss, when it claimed one of the Navy's few night kills. That evening, two F-4Js were performing single-ship off-shore MiGCAP in support of a 12-aeroplane Alpha strike launched from the *Saratoga* at dusk. Intelligence had told the crews that it believed an operational MiG-21 had been seen at Vinh (one of the VPAF's southernmost airfields) that day. Lt Cdr Robert E 'Gene' Tucker Jr and Lt(jg) Stanley B 'Bruce' Edens of VF-103 were flying the lead MiGCAP jet (BuNo 157299, call sign 'Clubleaf 206').

At 2018 hrs, *Red Crown* detected a bandit track south of Vinh, and immediately vectored Tucker's wing south-west to intercept. As the lead F-4J ingressed, Tucker's wing advised *Red Crown* that he was unable to locate the bandit with his radar. The controller recalled the jet, and vectored Tucker and Edens toward the 'bogey' instead. Their wing remained offshore, flying a route parallel with the coast.

Tucker and Edens approached the bandit, now confirmed as a MiG-21, on a south-westerly heading, and at 8000 ft. Tucker called 'Judy', which meant that the RIO, or pilot in the case of single-seat aircraft, had got total control of the intercept, including positioning for missile launch. It signified that the ground controller, or airborne intercept controller, should continue monitoring the intercept, but remain quiet while the RIO/pilot continued the intercept to missile launch, visual identification or whatever the rules of engagement required.

Having received clearance to fire from *Red Crown*, Tucker and Edens kept the MiG locked up. It was now ten degrees off their port side at just eight nautical miles. The pilot banked his Phantom II to the right on a 340-degree heading and fell into a trail position with the MiG, then increased his closure speed to 300 knots. The two held their pursuit for three minutes until Tucker lost his lock-on when the MiG-21 dropped to just 200 ft off the ground. At this point in the engagement, Tucker and Edens were about 130 nautical miles from Hanoi.

Tucker tried desperately to regain his lock on the MiG, descending to 3500 ft. Just after jettisoning his TERs and centreline tank, he reacquired the MiG dead-ahead, and low at six nautical miles. Tucker closed to within two nautical miles and centred his aim-dot, then triggered two AIM-7Es at four-second intervals. Both missiles guided and explosions were seen. At once, the contact dropped from both Edens' screen and from *Red Crown's*. Although neither crew member was able to locate the wreckage, the kill was officially confirmed two days later.

Seen ashore at NAS Oceana in the spring of 1973, this F-4J (BuNo 157305) features the kill marking of its assigned crew, squadron Operations Officer Lt Cdr Gene Tucker and RIO Lt(jg) Bruce Edens. As previously mentioned in this chapter, the crew were actually flying 'Clubleaf 206' (BuNo 157299) when they destroyed their MiG-21 on the night of 10 August 1972 (*via Brad Elward*)

With an empty TER just visible beneath the wing leading edge slats, 'Clubleaf 205' (BuNo 157303) nears the greasy deck of the *Saratoga* at the end of a bombing mission during *Linebacker I*. VF-103 and sister-squadron VF-31 were equipped with some of the newest F-4Js in the fleet just prior to their 1972-73 *WestPac* (*via Brad Elward*)

This engagement validated the tactic of flying a single-ship interception whilst undertaking a MiGCAP, as the authors of *Red Baron* explain;

'The tactics employed by *Red Crown* in directing this engagement were outstanding. The decision to immediately recall Tucker's lead when he was unable to establish radar contact enabled Tucker and Edens to conduct a successful intercept. *Red Crown's* foresight in directing Tucker's wing along the coast, parallel to the engagement, was another indication of excellent planning.

'The use of single-ship sorties at night is tactically sound. This procedure essentially created a free-fire zone for the attacker, while providing a viable back-up for the committed aircraft.'

Significantly, this engagement resulted in the Navy's sole AIM-7E Sparrow MiG kill of the entire *Linebacker* campaign.

EXCHANGE SUCCESS

Two days after this night kill, exchange pilot Capt Lawrence G Richard USMC and his RIO, Lt Cdr Michael J Ettel USN, scored a kill while flying Air Force F-4E 67-0239 (call sign 'Dodge 01') out of Udorn, Thailand, with the 58th Tactical Fighter Squadron/432nd Tactical Reconnaissance Wing.

The two naval aviators had sortied as the flight lead for a mixed formation of three F-4Es and an RF-4C on a weather reconnaissance mission in advance of *Linebacker* strikes scheduled for later that day. The mission called for photo-passes to be made over two targets – one just south-west of Yen Bai and the second on the Northeast Railway – coupled with the real-time collection of weather information using the RF-4C's high frequency radio.

The flight passed through the 'Gorilla's Head' then proceeded north across the Red River, about 115 nautical miles south-east of Yen Bai. As the flight crossed the river, *Red Crown* called, 'Bandits airborne out of *Bullseye*, heading 180 degrees'. However the flight proceeded on its mission 'to the middle of Thud Ridge at an altitude of 17,000 ft and at 450 knots, in fluid-four formation'.

Again, *Red Crown* called 'Bandits heading 210 degrees – turning to 360 degrees', then '"Blue bandits" (MiG-21s), bearing 180 degrees at 30 miles, accelerating at medium altitude'. The flight then slowed its speed to 300 knots, jettisoned its centreline tanks and accelerated back up to 450 knots. The flight began a left, descending turn, rolling out on a heading of 180 degrees. The MiGs were now directly ahead of the Phantom IIs, at 20 nautical miles. Closing, the flight selected minimum 'burner to conserve energy and reduce smoke trails. *Red Crown* then called, 'MiGs bearing 120 degrees at nine miles'. Capt Richard recounts what happened next;

'We spotted them at four miles just as they were starting their stern conversion on us. They were supersonic, while we were at 0.92 mach. I don't think they had acquired us visually, so they had to be relying on their GCI controller. The lead MiG-21 was silver, and his wingman was a mottled green camouflage – a really pretty aeroplane. I called tally ho, and we blew off our wing tanks as my element began a slice turn down into their inside. The MiGs had begun a slow port turn, which they hoped would put them at our "six o'clock". Our other element went high to protect my "six".

'At two miles I got a radar lock on the lead MiG-21. I don't think they had seen us yet, as their manoeuvres were not in the least bit evasive. As we closed to a mile-and-a-quarter, I fired a Sparrow. The missile came off the aeroplane and started leading out in front toward the MiG. I was about 20-30 degrees off his tail, and something must have told him to look back just then. He got the surprise of his life, because the Sparrow was about halfway to his aeroplane when he spotted it, and that big plume of smoke that it trails must have really gotten his adrenaline going. He reefed it right into me, and the missile went over the top of his aeroplane. I couldn't tell if it was really as close as it looked – if it was, then the fuse must have malfunctioned, because it didn't detonate.

'He passed me, canopy to canopy, no more than a couple of hundred feet away, rolled around my "six" and dove out of sight. As he did this,

Seen in November 1971, this 308th TFS/31st TFW aircraft was the sister-ship of 'MiG-killing' F-4E 67-0239, which was used by naval aviators Capt Lawrence Richard (USMC) and Lt Cdr Michael J Ettel (USN) to 'bag' a MiG-21 on 12 August 1972. Delivered to the USAF in May 1968, 67-0239 was initially issued to the 15th TFW at MacDill AFB, Florida, on 5 June 1968 as part of the wing's upgrade from the F-4C/D. On 16 January 1970 the fighter moved to the 560th TFS/4531st TFW at Homestead AFB, again in Florida. Nine months later, on 15 October, the 4531st was replaced by the 31st TFW. The 560th TFS was re-designated the 308th TFS (which formerly served with the 4403rd TFW) on 30 October. The squadron deployed (along with 67-0239) to Udorn Royal Thai Air Force Base on 1 May 1972 to operate on TDY (Temporary Duty) with the 432nd TRW. During its time in-theatre, 67-0239 was flown primarily by crews from the 308th until the squadron was replaced by the 307th TFS on 29 July. The F-4Es remained in-theatre, however, and it was used by an exchange crew from the 58th TFS to down a MiG-21 on 12 August 1972. The 58th was itself attached to the 432nd from the 33rd TFW! 67-0239 returned to Homestead on 31 October, and continued to serve with the 31st TFW post-war. In January 1980 it was one of 35 F-4Es taken from the 31st TFW and supplied to the Egyptian air force as part of Operation *Peace Pharoah*. 67-0239 still serves today with the 222nd Tactical Fighter Brigade at Quahira-West air base (*via Dave Menard*)

Lt Cdr Mike Ettel and Capt Larry Richard and their sharkmouthed F-4E 67-0239. Just how a crew of naval aviators got to down a MiG in a USAF jet is explained by Larry Richard. 'I was on exchange duty with the 58th TFS, out of Eglin AFB, Florida. We deployed to Udorn RTAFB for six months under what was termed the "Summer Help Program" in mid 1972. My back-seater was Lt Cdr Mike Ettel, who had been attached to the Air Force's 10th Weather Squadron at Udorn as a pilot. When the unit closed down operations, he was left without a job, so he went around to the various squadrons hoping to get assigned. Our squadron agreed to fly him in the back seat until he got current in the F-4, and he flew with me most of the time until he was qualified as an aircraft commander. That worked out well, since we were both on exchange duty with the Air Force.' Lt Cdr Ettel joined newly-formed adversary unit VF-43 at NAS Oceana in 1974, but his tenure with this unit did not last long, as double 'MiG killer' 'Mugs' McKeown explains. 'Mike Ettel was killed on 18 November 1974 when he had an engine flame out in TA-4J BuNo 154317 and couldn't get it restarted. When he tried to eject, the seat wouldn't fire, and he couldn't get the canopy to come off so he could get out manually. Mike just rode it in, broadcasting very calmly over the air to his wingman just before the jet went in the water, "Well, that's it. I'll see you guys"'

I unloaded my aeroplane, picked up some more speed and locked onto the wingman, who was still in his turn. His leader had just left him in the turn, and my high element assured me that the first MiG was smoking for home, and was no threat to me.

'I had pretty much the same parameters for firing at the second MiG, and I shot off another Sparrow. It came off the rail, smoked out in front of us, pulling lead on the MiG, and finally hit him just forward of the vertical fin. The MiG snapped up and rolled over into a spin as the tail fell off. I didn't see any big fireball or plume of smoke, and as I pulled up I lost sight of him.

'One of the funny aspects of the mission was that the recce pilot on my wing had no idea that we were going to engage the MiGs. When we turned around, he thought that we were just smoking for home. He had good reason to think so too, for recce flights were often chased out of North Vietnam by MiGs. The first indication that he had that things were not as he thought they should be was when wing tanks began coming off aeroplanes, and we went to full 'burner in a high-G turn. He was just hanging on for dear life, trying to keep from getting spat out of the rear end of the fight, and ending up on his own.

'Until he saw the Sparrows come off my aeroplane, he didn't know we were in a fight. He was as a happy with the results as I was though, and being a recce pilot, he took great delight in putting half a star on his intake ramp after the mission.'

MiG KILL

August was not all good for the Phantom II force, however, for on the 26th F-4J BuNo 155811 was lost to a MiG-21. At 1126 hrs, two F-4Js from Nam Phong-based VMFA-232 were flying BARCAP south of Hanoi is support of a large 101-aeroplane strike on the Xuan Mai military complex. What had started as a straightforward intercept quickly deteriorated when the fighters' radar control facility (codenamed *Teaball*, which was a newly-activated site not known for its reliability) failed as the F-4s closed on the MiGs. Problems were further exacerbated by a faulty radio in one of the Marine jets.

By the time *Red Crown* could pass radar vectors to the BARCAP, the MiGs had passed the F-4s, and six-kill ace Lt Nguyen Duc Soat of the 927th Fighter Regiment fired off an Atoll at 1Lts Sam Cordova and D L Borders in a 'high-speed, one-pass' attack. The Marine jet was struck in the tail by the AA-2, and it was quickly consumed by fire.

Both crewmen ejected, and although 1Lt Cordova communicated with other aircraft in the area on his survival radio, he was killed either during or after capture. 1Lt Borders enjoyed better luck, however, being rescued by a USAF HH-53 helicopter.

Aside from the crucial radar failure, another contributing factor that led to this loss were the poor tactics employed by the lead Marine jet. 1Lt Borders said;

'All through the intercept, after about 20 miles' range, I just wanted to get the hell out. It was obvious that if we engaged we would be extremely lucky to even get out, much less bag a MiG. When lead went into a shallow, left descending turn, I knew that if the MiGs saw us, we were definitely on the defensive, and at a big disadvantage. Our flight failed to do the basics – we didn't punch tanks, no AB (afterburner), poor communications, lack of aggressiveness etc. We entered the fight on the defensive rather than on the offensive.'

The only MiG kill credited to a Marine Corps crew in a Marine Corps jet fell to VMFA-333 during the unit's 1972-73 *WestPac* aboard the USS *America* (CVA-66). This photograph shows a number of 'Shamrock' crews relaxing between sorties in the unit's ready room aboard the carrier. All of these men each had over 200 landings on CVA-66 to their names when this shot was taken in late 1972. Standing at the extreme left is Maj 'Bear' Lasseter, XO of the unit (later promoted to CO after Lt Col John Cochran had to return to the US for hospital treatment after ejecting from his battle damaged F-4 on 23 December 1972), and the pilot who 'bagged' VMFA-333's MiG. His RIO on this mission, Capt 'Lil' John Cummings, can be seen kneeling (right) (*via Peter E Davies*)

Just two weeks later, though, VMFA-333 restored some pride to the Marine Corps when two F-4Js intercepted two MiG-21s over Phuc Yen, destroying one and damaging the other. The squadron was operating with CVW-8 aboard the *America* at the time, its participation in this *WestPac* cruise marking the first time that a Marine F-4 squadron had deployed aboard a Navy carrier.

On 11 September, Marine Corps Topgun graduates Maj Lee T 'Bear' Lasseter (VMFA-333's XO) and Capt John D 'Lil' John' Cummings were flying lead in BuNo 155526, call sign 'Shamrock 201', with Capt 'Scotty' Dudley and 1Lt 'Diamond Jim' Brady in BuNo 154784, calls sign 'Shamrock 206, as their wing. They were part of a four-ship MiGCAP sortied to protect an Alpha strike sent to bomb the Co Giam SAM assembly area about 50 nautical miles north-east of Hanoi.

The remainder of the strike package consisted of seven A-7 Corsairs and four A-6 Intruders, each carrying Mk 82 500-lb 'iron' bombs, four *Iron Hand* A-7s and four F-4Js configured for flak suppression. Each of the MiGCAP Phantom IIs were armed with four AIM-7E-2 Sparrows and four AIM-9G Sidewinders, plus a 600-gallon centreline tank.

According to official reports, the MiGCAP crews had been briefed to perform a pre-strike weather check of the primary and secondary target areas, then relay their findings before the strike package crossed the beach. As part of this MiGCAP, Lasseter and Cummings and their wing were in the process of tanking when *Red Crown* noted that the strike package was just six miles away. The section was immediately instructed to disengage and commence their run, preceding the main force to their coast-in point. Lasseter and Cummings were at 6000 ft, and their wing was at 9000 ft.

Upon reaching the coast in point, Lasseter's section was vectored, 'Bandits, 290 for 61'. The pilot of 'Shamrock 201' noted after the mission, 'We came west to 290 degrees and started a nice descent which ended up at about 3500-4000 ft'. The two contacts – MiG-21s – were orbiting near Phuc Yen airfield at approximately 12,000 ft.

Red Crown called again, 'Bandits at 268 degrees for 28'. Now, a second group of bandits appeared (two-to-four MiGs) coming out of the north-west towards Phuc Yen. Lasseter added, 'At this time we began to realise that this was not an average day. We were going into a big trap. We were looking right into the sun, and the "bogies" were repeatedly changing altitudes. We had numerous contacts with the MiGs, but couldn't get a lock-up because as soon as they turned head on, we lost them'.

When *Red Crown* called the bandits at 12 nautical miles, the two F-4 pilots selected afterburner and continued on their attack vector.

When the section reached a position a few miles to the east of Phuc Yen, Capt Dudley sighted two MiG-21s at his '11 o'clock', some seven nautical miles away. The trailing MiG, painted light blue, was out to the left and high on the lead MiG, which was unpainted. Lasseter also saw the MiGs and started an attack. As he later recalled, 'I picked up the lead MiG and locked him up. As soon as I had done this, the wingman decided to leave'.

Cummings reported, 'As far as the radar goes, this guy was in orbit, and that ruled out pulse Doppler radar, so everything was in pulse. We don't have an automatic angle track for boresight in our particular aircraft, just an extended switch. This really helps out because you just slap it down and you're in boresight. As soon as you get a lock-on, just slap it back up again, and you have angle lock. We locked the MiG up with this technique.

'At three nautical miles, locked-up with a clearance to shoot from *Red Crown*, we committed one missile. I waited too long for the missile to come off and committed another. We lost two AIM-7E-2s right there. The missiles came off and started toward the MiG. It looked like good guidance, but the MiG made a square corner. He

'Shamrock 203' forms up with its strike lead and heads for North Vietnam in the summer of 1972. The aircraft's offensive weaponry consists of six Mk 82 500-lb low drag bombs, four AIM-9G Sidewinders and two AIM-7E-2 Sparrows. The clean appearance of this aircraft suggests that it was photographed soon after CVA-66 arrived on the line on 14 July 1972 (*via Robert F Dorr*)

Less immaculate than the jet seen above, a storeless 'Shamrock 207' is connected to waist catapult three in preparation for launching. Note the *Mickey Mouse* head that adorns the splitter plate of the VF-74 jet secured to waist catapult four (*via Peter E Davies*)

rotated from a rear quarter to a beam aspect, just like that. That, of course, put our speed-gate into the ground clutter, and that's where, I presume, our missiles locked-on. The missiles never saw him when they came off the aircraft.'

Through four to five turns, both Phantom IIs and the MiG leader maintained full afterburner in a maximum rate, left, descending ('graveyard spiral') turn. Pulling between 4-7G, Lasseter was trying to manoeuvre on the MiG by using the vertical plane to lag-roll to the outside in preparation for another missile shot. He achieved a position at the MiG's 'six' at an altitude of 3000 ft, and less than a mile range, and triggered an AIM-9G. However, the missile detonated about 1000 ft in front of his aircraft.

'It (the missile that detonated early) damned near cost me a quarter of a turn on the MiG', Lasseter noted. 'I continued using the vertical and watching him – I didn't take my eyes off the MiG. Any time we got into a really good position to shoot, from here on out we'd get SAM-launch indications. My RIO was pumping out chaff as fast as he could, and we were turning as hard as we could'.

Still having a full-system lock-on, Lasseter triggered off a second AIM-9G. 'I shot a Sidewinder which went ballistic, although it was fired in parameters. We were just fixing to break away and go home because the MiG was in a left turn, just above the tree-tops, and there was no way to get him now. I committed two more Sparrows, however, with a high-clutter environment'.

When the lead MiG pilot saw that these two missiles had missed, he reversed his turn and allowed Lasseter to fire a third AIM-9G from the 'six o'clock' position, level, at an altitude of about 1000 ft, with one-half to three-quarters of a mile separation. This missile detonated in the MiG's tailpipe and severed its aft section just behind the canopy.

As Lasseter passed over the MiG's fireball, he looked up and saw a black-nosed MiG-21 (his victim's wingman) making a high, descending pass on Dudley. Lasseter quickly called for Dudley to 'break', which caused the MiG to overshoot. Dudley then reversed and Lasseter fired an AIM-9G from the MiG's 'six o'clock'. Seconds later, the VPAF jet took evasive action by dispensing a decoy flare. Lasseter said the flare was 'about half the intensity of a Mk-45 (a standard US night flare)'.

'The Sidewinder had no hesitation at all', Lasseter explained. 'It went straight to the MiG. It did not go for the decoy flare'. This missile hit the MiG's aft fuselage area, causing the jet to smoke. The MiG disengaged, then made a gradual high-speed, descending turn to depart the area. Dudley, now reaching a critically low fuel state, fired a final AIM-7E-2, but by then the MiG was out of range.

'Lil John' Cummings and 'Bear' Lasseter pose with their weapon of choice the day after downing their MiG-21 on 11 September 1972. These two individuals formed *the* crack F-4 crew within CVW-8 during CVA-66's combat cruise. Both men had already completed combat tours in Vietnam with land-based Marine Phantom II units, and had first crewed up as instructors in 1969 when assigned to the Marine Air Weapons Training Unit. Cummings had gone on to receive the USMC Naval Flight Officer of the Year Award in 1971 for developing 'Aircrew coordination techniques which allow the F-4 RIO to virtually fly the aircraft through directions to the pilot, when the pilot is visually unable to acquire the target', as well as 'Tactics which allow fighter aircraft to approach enemy aircraft undetected with all weapons simultaneously brought to bear'. Cummings had also published numerous articles on fighter tactics, which were considered 'The 2nd Marine Aircraft Wing's basis for the tactical deployment of the F-4 on long-range escort, night escort, BARCAP and TARCAP missions'. Together, Lasseter and Cummings led VMFA-333's ACM effort. Described by RIO Cummings as a 'gentle warrior', 'Bear' Lasseter passed away during routine surgery in 1981 (*via Robert F Dorr*)

Seen at MCAS Beaufort in early 1970, BuNo 155526 was the F-4J used by Lasseter and Cummings to destroy their MiG-21. Accepted by the Navy at St Louis on 8 February 1968 and transferred to VF-103 six days later, the fighter served with the 'Sluggers' for just a matter of weeks, for on 25 March it left Oceana and headed south to Beaufort to join VMFA-333 – the unit was in the process of replacing its F-8Es at the time. BuNo 155526 participated in two cruises with the unit aboard the *America*, the first of these being a Mediterranean deployment in 1970. On 5 June 1972 VMFA-333 once again joined up with CVA-66 and headed for Vietnam. On 11 September it claimed one MiG-21 destroyed and a second example damaged, before being lost to a SAM (*via R F Dorr*)

Cummings and Lasseter with the two MiG kill symbols that were applied to the replacement 'Shamrock 201' (BuNo 155852). Unofficially they were allowed 1.5 kills, but officially just one (*via Peter E Davies*)

As the section began egress, Lasseter called for a fuel check – he had 2200 lbs while Dudley reported, 1700 lbs. Lasseter advised Dudley to 'Keep it leaned out'.

During their egress, both crews heard continuous SAM-launch and AAA warnings. Because they had expended all of their chaff during the MiG engagement, Lasseter and Dudley wanted to bypass as much of the heavy ground defences as possible. Therefore, the pilot of 'Shamrock 201' selected a route to the north of Ile Cac Ba.

Passing just north of Haiphong at 15,000 ft, the Phantom IIs turned onto a heading of 160-170 degrees to rendezvous with their tankers, which were about 25 nautical miles away. During this turn, Dudley saw a SA-2 pass about 20 ft below Lasseter and continue up to about 25,000 ft, where it detonated. He saw a second SAM about 300 yards to Lasseter's rear, which detonated within a few feet of his leader's tail.

Lasseter later declared, 'If you ever get hit by a SAM there's no doubt about it. It's a 500-lb bomb going off right at your tailpipe. We immediately had two fire lights, and everything in the cockpit was going ape. We lost all our hydraulic fluid, and we were on fire'.

Even though his jet was seriously damaged by the SAM, Lasseter was nevertheless able to maintain control of the F-4 by slowing down. He continued egress to about 15 nautical miles 'feet-wet'. During this time, an unidentified F-4 heading 150 degrees at 15,000 ft was sighted by the tankers – the tankers turned 150 degrees to rendezvous. This turn delayed the rendezvous with Lasseter's section such that when they reached the tanking point both were registering 'zero fuel remaining' readings.

Just as Dudley reported that 'Shamrock 201' was 'burning pretty bad', Lasseter lost control of his aircraft. 'I said, "Okay, let's go", took my hand off the stick, and reached for the alternate handle. That was a big mistake! The aeroplane departed into an inverted spin and we had about 4-6 negative G on us. We fought like SOBs to get out of that aeroplane. It was close to me not being here today.'

Following Lasseter's example, Dudley also ejected. All four crew members were recovered. A later study of the mission cockpit tape revealed that both Phantom IIs had been operating in maximum afterburner for just under six minutes. Both had about 9000 lbs of fuel at the time of afterburner initiation, which was consistent with the 2200 and 1700 lbs disengagement fuel readings. *Red Baron* pedantically concluded that both crews had erred in continuing their engagement until they had insufficient fuel to egress safely.

By October, the North had expended its supply of missiles, and was miserably short of anti-aircraft ammunition. American aircraft roamed at large, unmolested as they had in the last days of the war in Europe. But at the very point where the US had seemingly defeated the North Vietnamese, Operation *Linebacker I* was terminated. On 23 October, President Nixon called a bombing halt north of the 20th Parallel, bringing to an end the most successful bombing campaign of the war.

LINEBACKER II

Operation *Linebacker II* began on 18 December 1972 when negotiations at the heart of the Paris Peace Talks appeared to stagnate. Called the 'Christmas Bombings' by some, these raids saw the most intense air assault on North Vietnam of the entire war. Directed by the Joint Chiefs of Staff, the strikes were maximum effort missions intended to hastily force the North Vietnamese back to the negotiating table, where a cease-fire agreement could be signed.

The heaviest air strikes took place during an 11-day period in late December that saw both Hanoi and Haiphong bombed, although air activity continued below the 20th parallel until 16 January, when all bombing of North Vietnam was halted.

On 28 December, the Navy claimed its first MiG kill of the *Linebacker II* campaign, when an F-4J (BuNo 155846, call sign 'Dakota 214') from *Enterprise's* VF-142 downed a MiG-21 during an Alpha strike on the Hanoi Radio Station, six nautical miles south of the city. The total force consisted of 12 strike aircraft, supported by reconnaissance, CAP and *Iron Hand* sorties.

A section of two F-4Js from VF-142, one of which was crewed by Lt(jg)s Scott H Davis and Geoffrey H 'Jeff' Ulrich, was assigned MiGCAP duty in support of the strike. The Phantom IIs ingressed from the south, coasting in near Thanh Hoa, and proceeding north to their assigned CAP point some 30 nautical miles south of Hanoi. The MiGCAP was to refuel and ingress early to perform a weather reconnaissance prior to the strike force's arrival. However, a deck foul-up delayed the tanker and necessitated the flight's ingress without refuelling. The Phantom IIs had no more than 11,000 lbs of fuel when they passed Thanh Hoa, inbound.

The flight reached its assigned CAP orbit with only light defensive reactions (some generally inaccurate 85 mm AAA), and began orbiting the CAP point at 10,000 ft and 350 knots. After two to three turns in the

No photographs of Scott Davis and Jeff Ulrich's 'MiG-killing' F-4J (BuNo 155846) have so far come to light, although this shot of 'Dakota 205' (BuNo 155764) shows how VF-142's Phantom IIs were marked for the unit's seventh, and last, Vietnam deployment. This photo was taken at NAS Miramar soon after the unit had returned home in June 1973. The Battle Efficiency 'E' and Safety 'S' worn on the jet's splitter plate were applied to all squadron aircraft after VF-142 had arrived back in southern California (*via Brad Elward*)

pattern, *Red Crown* called that a 'Blue Bandit' (MiG-21) was launching out of Hanoi.

A subsequent call placed the MiG five nautical miles east of Hanoi, at which time Davis's lead requested an intercept vector from *Red Crown*. However, no vectors were issued (*Red Crown* did not have radar contact with the bandit). The fighter controller called again, now indicating that the MiG was seven nautical miles north of the inbound strike group. Davis's section was then directed to a new heading of 010 degrees. The strike group was now north of the CAP point, and between the two F-4s and the approaching MiG.

As the Phantom IIs accelerated to the north at 10,000 ft, retaining their empty centreline tanks, RIO Ulrich began searching for the MiG with his radar. 'It was a hopeless situation', Ulrich commented. 'We were painting about ten aeroplanes (the strike force) on every sweep, and there was no way of telling which one might be the bandit. Finally, I gave up any hope of a long-range radar shot and just went 100 per cent visual'.

Davis takes up the account. 'In just a few seconds, I picked up a MiG-21 about 10,000 ft high and three to four miles out. He was in the rear quadrant of what appeared to be an F-4, and the sun was glinting off his canopy. I called for my lead to turn left, and I too started left after the MiG'. Interestingly, Davis's lead heard the call, but did not understand it. But when he saw his wingman turning left, he followed him in fighting-wing formation.

'As I turned left, the MiG turned left toward me, still in pursuit of the other F-4, but apparently unaware of us. We continued the climb at 376 knots in military power and, as we approached about 90 degrees angle-off on the bandit, he reversed his turn to the right. He rolled out right in front of me! I put the pipper on his tailpipe and got a good tone on the Sidewinder.'

Davis then noticed that he was right in the middle of several F-4s. 'The F-4s were weaving, and the MiG was jinking back and forth, trying to get into position. I was afraid to fire for fear of hitting a friendly. In my line-of-sight, the MiG was superimposed on an American aircraft. It seemed that because of the difference in size, the friendly must have then been behind the bandit. I saw a missile come off one of the aeroplanes, but it didn't hit anyone. Then another missile came off and there was a huge explosion. I remember thinking, "That was no MiG blowing up – the explosion is too big"'.

What Davis did not know then was that the exploding aircraft was RA-5C BuNo 156633 of RVAH-13, also embarked in the *Enterprise*. Hit by an Atoll, the aircraft burst into flames, and only the pilot (Lt Cdr Alfred Agnew) succeeded in ejecting. This ill-fated Vigilante was the 90th, and last, US aircraft to be shot down by a VPAF MiG according to official American sources.

'I told *Red Crown* that someone had been downed, and a SAR was required, as I chased after the MiG in his left, descending turn to disengage', Davis added. 'It appeared obvious that he was headed for the cloud deck about five miles away'.

Remaining in military power, Davis (with his lead now in fighting wing) cut across the inside of the MiG's turn to close the range. 'I knew I had to get him to turn into me to prevent him reaching the clouds, so I put

'Dakota 201' (BuNo 155894) served as the CO's aircraft with VF-142 during the unit's 1972-73 *WestPac* aboard the *Enterprise*. 'MiG killer' BuNo 155846 was delivered to the Navy on 23 January 1969, just months prior to this particular aircraft. Issued to VF-121 on 12 February, BuNo 155846 joined VF-142 at Miramar 16 days later, the aircraft being transferred to the unit as a replacement for one of its war-weary F-4Bs. It completed single *WestPac*/Vietnam cruises with the unit, as part of CVW-14, aboard the *Constellation* (August 1969 to May 1970) and *Enterprise* (June 1971 to February 1972), before returning to TF-77 with CVAN-65 in September 1972. On 28 December BuNo 155846's 'nugget' crew of Scott Davis and Jeff Ulrich downed a MiG-21. The jet was destined not to survive its third *WestPac*, however, for on 3 May 1973 it crashed at sea after its crew suffered 'control problems' – there is no other information available on this accident. BuNo 155846 had completed 1395 flight hours by the time of its premature demise (*via Mike France*)

the pipper on him and fired an AIM-9 with about 75 degrees angle-off. The missile guided and blew up just behind the MiG. It apparently didn't damage him, but he sure pulled it back into me hard. We continued to spiral down the inside of his turn, and my RIO advised me that my lead was beginning to slide forward toward my "nine o'clock" low position. I looked out to the left, past lead, and saw another F-4 about a mile out, headed toward us. Just as I picked him up, he fired a missile'.

Davis assumed that the F-4 was firing at the MiG. Consequently, he was not concerned about the missile. Later, Davis learned that his lead's RIO had also seen the missile and called to his pilot to 'break'. Honouring the call, lead broke and lost sight of Davis. The missile passed between the two Phantom IIs. 'Seeing the MiG duck into a little hole in the clouds', Davis recalls, 'I plugged in the 'burners and pressed after him, popping into the clouds in about a 45-degree dive. We broke out of the bottom at about 100 ft and 640 knots.

'I reacquired the MiG almost immediately, about 40 degrees off to the left. I guess he saw us at the same time, because he pulled hard into us. I let the nose lag a little and then pulled it around toward his tail again. I'd just gotten the pipper back to his tail when he reversed back to the left.

'I got a good tone on him then, and squeezed off another AIM-9. This one was tracking okay, but the MiG went through a little wisp of low-hanging cloud and the missile lost him and went ballistic. We were down to about 50 ft by this time, and we just kept chasing him back and forth in a not-too-vigorous horizontal scissors.

'I was gradually getting more and more in phase with him, and the range was down to about 3000 ft. I eventually set myself up to where I had a good tone at the beginning of his reversal, and as he rolled right to reverse, I fired another AIM-9. When he turned far enough to be able to see the missile, he really pulled it hard, and the missile went off about ten feet behind him with no apparent damage.'

A few seconds after the missile went off Davis saw the MiG's nose yaw up about 20 degrees, hesitate, and then yaw down about the same amount. 'He oscillated again', Davis related. 'The nose came a little higher this time, hesitated, and then started back down. It continued to drop to about 50 degrees, and he just ploughed into the ground in a big ball of fire.

'We passed over the top of him about two miles south of Hanoi, and started receiving some really heavy 23 mm AAA. I came hard right and began to jink out at 50 ft and 600 knots, between 090 and 120 degrees. I called my lead, who was just about over our position on top of the clouds, and told him we were egressing. Passing the beach, we zoomed to about 16,000 ft and got vectored to the tanker. We hooked up with 2900 lbs.'

Little harm was done to 'Dakota 207' (BuNo 155888) when its pilot (Lt Bruyere) was forced to take the barricade after his jet suffered flak damage over North Vietnam on 3 November 1972. VF-142 did not lose a single jet to enemy action during its final wartime cruise, although 'MiG killer' BuNo 155846 was of course destroyed in an operational accident whilst operating over the Gulf of Tonkin on 3 May 1973 (via Peter Mersky)

Second only to VF-96 in the number of MiGs it claimed during the Vietnam War, VF-161 proudly marked all of its F-4Bs with the legend THE MIG KILLERS on their splitter plates, as well as a red silhouette of a MiG-17, onto which the number '5' had been sprayed – the unit's tally on its final cruise. One aircraft so decorated was 'Rock River 113' (BuNo 151453), seen here on the Miramar ramp following VF-161's return from Vietnam in March 1973 (via Brad Elward)

The two Phantom IIs rejoined on the post-strike tanker and the section returned to the ship without further incident.

FINAL KILL

On 12 January 1973, the Navy claimed its 57th and last MiG of the war when two F-4Bs from VF-161 engaged and shot down a MiG-17 over the Gulf of Tonkin, some 55 miles south-east of Haiphong.

At about 1330 hrs, Lt Victor T Kovaleski and his RIO, Lt(jg) James A Wise, were flying a routine fleet-defence BARCAP mission (in BuNo 153045, call sign 'Rock River 102') from the *Midway* when they were directed by *Red Crown* to intercept an unknown contact. Kovaleski's section complied, but was then ordered to 'break off' the engagement. A few moments later, the section was again vectored onto an unknown blip, only to again be ordered to break off the intercept.

As Kovaleski's centreline tank went dry, his section was again given an intercept vector. This time, however, *Red Crown* had a position radar contact, and vectored the two Phantom IIs onto a north-east heading. Immediately, Kovaleski's wing assumed a combat-spread formation, 1500 ft high and 3000 ft out, line-abreast of him.

As the range to the MiG closed, Kovaleski and Wise descended to 3000 ft and accelerated to approximately 450 knots. At a range of four nautical miles, the pilot of 'Rock River 102' called a visual contact of a dark-coloured MiG-17, heading north at 500 ft. Obtaining clearance to

fire, the section closed to less than one mile of the MiG's 'seven o'clock'. At that moment, the VPAF pilot broke hard to the left, then into Kovaleski and Wise. The section slid into the MiG's 'six o'clock' blind spot, but anticipating an overshoot, the MiG pilot reversed hard to his right.

Still maintaining good nose-tail separation, Kovaleski and Wise reversed right with the MiG, placing it within the piper. Kovaleski triggered a Sidewinder, which detonated behind the MiG, knocking off a section of its tail. But the fighter kept flying.

Kovaleski triggered a second Sidewinder, this one at a range of 3000 ft. The missile guided well, and just before its impact, the crew saw the North Vietnamese pilot eject. The MiG then exploded in a huge fireball and careened into the water. No 'chute was seen. Kovaleski said after the engagement that 'the MiG made it easy for me by reversing back to the right prior to my overshooting – he solved the problem'.

Red Baron's review of the engagement concluded, 'Good flight discipline, excellent control by *Red Crown* and missiles that performed properly, all combined to achieve this clean kill – the last kill in the Southeast Asian air war. Shit Hot!' The report ended, 'We finally got it right'.

VF-161's kill was indeed the 167th and last MiG victory of the war. It was also *Midway's* fifth MiG of the *Linebacker* campaign.

In an interesting twist, Lt Kovaleski also held the dubious honour of piloting the last American aircraft to be lost over North Vietnam when he and his RIO, Ens D H Plautz (flying F-4B BuNo 153068, call sign 'Rock River 110' – this aircraft had been credited with a MiG kill on 18 May 1972), were downed by AAA over North Vietnam on 14 January while on a *Blue Tree* escort mission near Thanh Hoa. Both men were recovered by a Navy HH-3A SAR helicopter after ejecting over the sea.

US air operations in South-east Asia formally came to an end on 27 January 1973 following the signing of an armistice agreement by the North Vietnamese, the Viet Cong, South Vietnam and the Americans in Paris.

Linebacker had seen naval fighter crews unequivocally re-establish themselves as MiG masters. Indeed, the Navy's kill-to-loss ratio stood at a dramatic 12.5-to-1, with naval F-4s downing 25 VPAF MiGs for the loss of just two ship-based Phantom IIs. This obviously compared well with the overall service rate during the entire war of 2.13 MiGs downed for every aircraft lost to VPAF fighters. Clearly, Navy aircrews had reacquired the skills that they had once exhibited in the skies over the Pacific.

Parked alongside 'Rock River 113' at Miramar in March 1973 was the Navy's final 'MiG killer', F-4B BuNo 153045. Delivered on 17 August 1966, the jet initially served at NAS Key West with VF-101, where it remained until 30 November 1966. Then transferred to VF-74 at Oceana, it completed the unit's pre-Vietnam work-ups but was transferred to Miramar in June 1967. Without a unit until October, the fighter then joined VF-114, and participated in the unit's 1967-68 *WestPac*/Vietnam deployment aboard the *Kitty Hawk*. BuNo 153045 returned to TF-77 again aboard CVA-63 in December 1968, this cruise lasting until September 1969. In July 1970 the fighter transferred to VF-161, and it served with the 'Chargers' through to July 1973. In that time it completed two *WestPac*/Vietnam deployments aboard the *Midway*, the first between April and November 1971, and the second from April 1972 to March 1973. Placed in storage at NARF North Island in August 1973, the fighter was upgraded into an F-4N in 1974-75. BuNo 153045 was then issued to VF-301 at Miramar, and it continued to serve with the reserve unit until April 1981. Passed on to H&MS-41 'Det Dallas', which was parented by reserve-manned VMFA-112, the aircraft became permanently controlled by the 'Cowboys' in October 1981. Retired by the unit in September 1983 following VMFA-112's re-equipment with the F-4S, BuNo 153045 was administratively stricken on the 7th of that month, having completed 4213 flight hours. Its final disposition is unknown (*via Elward*)

APPENDICES

US NAVY/MARINE CORPS F-4 PHANTOM II MiG KILLERS 1972-73

Date	Squadron	BuNo	Crew	Carrier/Air Wing	Aircraft	Weapon
19/1/72	VF-96	157267	R Cunningham W Driscoll	Constellation/CVW-9	MiG-21	AIM-9
6/3/72	VF-111	153019	G Weigand W Freckleton	Coral Sea/CVW-15	MiG-17	AIM-9
6/5/72	VF-51	150456	J Houston K Moore	Coral Sea/CVW-15	MiG-17	AIM-9
6/5/72	VF-114	157249	R Hughes K Moore	Kitty Hawk/CVW-11	MiG-21	AIM-9
6/5/72	VF-114	157245	K Pettigrew M McCabe	Kitty Hawk/CVW-11	MiG-21	AIM-9
8/5/72	VF-96	157267	R Cunningham W Driscoll	Constellation/CVW-9	MiG-17	AIM-9
10/5/72	VF-92	157269	C Dosé J McDevitt	Constellation/CVW-9	MiG-21	AIM-9
10/5/72	VF-96	155769	M Connelly T Blonski	Constellation/CVW-9	MiG-17	AIM-9
10/5/72	VF-96	155769	M Connelly T Blonski	Constellation/CVW-9	MiG-17	AIM-9
10/5/72	VF-51	151398	K Cannon R Morris	Coral Sea/CVW-15	MiG-17	AIM-9
10/5/72	VF-96	155749	S Shoemaker K Crenshaw	Constellation/CVW-9	MiG-17	AIM-9
10/5/72	VF-96	155800	R Cunningham W Driscoll	Constellation/CVW-9	MiG-17	AIM-9
10/5/72	VF-96	155800	R Cunningham W Driscoll	Constellation/CVW-9	MiG-17	AIM-9
10/5/72	VF-96	155800	R Cunningham W Driscoll	Constellation/CVW-9	MiG-17	AIM-9
18/5/72	VF-161	153068	H Bartholomay O Brown	Midway/CVW-5	MiG-19	AIM-9
18/5/72	VF-161	153915	P Arwood J Bell	Midway/CVW-5	MiG-19	AIM-9
23/5/72	VF-161	153020	R McKeown J Ensch	Midway/CVW-5	MiG-17	AIM-9
23/5/72	VF-161	153020	R McKeown J Ensch	Midway/CVW-5	MiG-17	AIM-9
11/6/72	VF-51	149473	F Teague R Howell	Coral Sea/CVW-15	MiG-17	AIM-9
11/6/72	VF-51	149457	W Copeland D Bouchoux	Coral Sea/CVW-15	MiG-17	AIM-9
21/6/72	VF-31	157307	S Flynn W John	Saratoga/CVW-3	MiG-21	AIM-9
10/8/72	VF-103	157299	R Tucker S Edens	Saratoga/CVW-3	MiG-21	AIM-7
12/8/72	58th TFS/432nd TRW	67-0239	L Richard M Ettel	Udorn RTAB	MiG-21	AIM-7
11/9/72	VMFA-333	155526	L Lasseter J Cummings	America/CVW-8	MiG-21	AIM-9
28/12/72	VF-142	155846	S Davis G Ulrich	Enterprise/CVW-14	MiG-21	AIM-9
12/1/73	VF-161	153045	V Kovaleski J Wise	Midway/CVW-5	MiG-17	AIM-9

COLOUR PLATES

Editor's Note: Due to a restriction on space in this volume, the plates commentaries for the colour profiles appear in point form. Further information on most of these aeroplanes appears within the photo captions throughout the book.

1
F-4J BuNo 157267/NG 112 of Lt Randall H Cunningham and Lt(jg) William P Driscoll, VF-96, USS *Constellation*, 19 January and 8 May 1972
Delivered – 13 January 1970
Units served with – VF-121, VF-96, VF-114, VF-21, VMFA-232, VMFA-235, VMFA-122
Major modifications – upgraded to F-4S in 1979-80
Final fate – on display in the San Diego Aerospace Museum, California, since March 1990

2
F-4B BuNo 153019/NL 201 of Lt Garry L Weigand and Lt(jg) William C Freckleton, VF-111, USS *Coral Sea*, 6 March 1972
Delivered – 5 May 1966
Units served with – VF-213, VF-121, VF-111, VMFA-531, VF-201, VF-171
Major modifications – upgraded to F-4N in 1976
Final fate – gate guard at NAS Key West, Florida

3
F-4B BuNo 150456/NL 100 of Lt Cdr Jerry B Houston and Lt Kevin T Moore, VF-51, USS *Midway*, 6 May 1972
Delivered – 6 December 1962
Units served with – VF-121, VF-151, VF-161, VF-143, VF-51, VF-41, VF-301, VMFA-321
Major modifications – upgraded to F-4N in 1973-74
Final fate – expended as a QF-4N target drone in a missile test at the Naval Weapons Center at China Lake, in California, on 27 January 1989

4
F-4J BuNo 157249/NH 206 of Lt Robert G Hughes and Lt(jg) Adolph J Cruz, VF-114, USS *Kitty Hawk*, 6 May 1972
Delivered – 6 October 1969
Units served with – VF-114, VF-21, VMFA-212, VMFA-235, VMFA-122, VF-33, VF-103, VF-171, VMFA-115, VMFAT-101, VMFA-212
Major modifications – upgraded to F-4S in 1981-82
Final fate – stored since October 1986 in AMARC's Davis-Monthan facility

5
F-4J BuNo 157245/NH 201 of Lt Cdr Kenneth W Pettigrew and Lt(jg) Michael J McCabe, VF-114, USS *Kitty Hawk*, 6 May 1972
Delivered – 24 September 1969
Units served with – VF-114, VF-51, VMFA-212, VMFA-232, VF-121, VF-103, VMFA-251
Major modifications – upgraded to F-4S in 1980-81
Final fate – stored since August 1985 in AMARC's Davis-Monthan facility

6
F-4J BuNo 157269/NG 211 of Lt Curt Dosé and Lt Cdr James McDevitt, VF-92, USS *Constellation*, 10 May 1972
Delivered – 5 February 1970
Units served with – VF-121, VF-92, VF-114, VMFAT-101, VMFA-235
Major modifications – upgraded to F-4S in 1979-80
Final fate – stored since February 1986 in AMARC's Davis-Monthan facility

7
F-4J BuNo 155769/NG 106 of Lt Michael J Connelly and Lt Thomas J J Blonski, VF-96, USS *Constellation*, 10 May 1972
Delivered – 27 July 1968
Units served with – VF-154, VF-142, VF-121, VF-96, VF-194, VF-302
Major modifications – upgraded to F-4S in 1980-81
Final fate – crashed during landing roll-out at NAS Dallas, Texas, on 4 April 1983, both crewmen ejecting safely

8
F-4B BuNo 151398/NL 111 of Lt Kenneth L Cannon and Lt Roy A Morris, VF-51, USS *Coral Sea*, 10 May 1972
Delivered – 2 August 1963
Units served with – VF-101, VF-102, VF-32, VF-142, VMFA-115, VF-51, VF-161,
Major modifications – upgraded to F-4N in 1972-73
Final fate – scrapped in Tucson, Arizona, in 1990

9
F-4J BuNo 155749/NG 111 of Lt Steven C Shoemaker and Lt(jg) Keith V Crenshaw, VF-96, USS *Constellation*, 10 May 1972
Delivered – 24 June 1968
Units served with – VF-21, VF-142, VF-96, VMFA-212, VMFAT-101, VMFA-235, VF-301, VMFA-321, VMFA-134
Major modifications – upgraded to F-4S in 1979-80
Final fate – converted into a QF-4S, the jet was lost during the annual Point Mugu airshow on 20 April 2002 whilst serving with the Naval Weapons Test Squadron. It crashed due to an apparent engine malfunction just before it was due to land after its demonstration flight. Both crewmen were killed.

10
F-4J BuNo 155800/NG 100 of Lt Randall H Cunningham and Lt(jg) William P Driscoll, VF-96, USS *Constellation*, 10 May 1972
Delivered – 17 October 1968
Unit served with – VF-96
Major modifications – none
Final fate – damaged by a SAM and crew ejected off North Vietnamese coastline on 10 May 1972

11
F-4B BuNo 153068/NF 110 of Lt Henry A

Bartholomay and Lt Oran R Brown, VF-161, USS *Midway*, 18 May 1972
Delivered – 4 November 1966
Units served with – VF-74, VF-11, VF-213, the *Blue Angels*, VF-161
Major modifications – none
Final fate – damaged by AAA and the crew (including MiG-killing pilot Lt Victor Kovaleski) forced to eject over the Gulf of Tonkin on 14 January 1973

12

F-4B BuNo 153915/NF 105 of Lt Patrick E Arwood and Lt James M Bell, VF-161, USS *Midway*, 18 May 1972
Delivered – 30 November 1966
Units served with – VF-121, VF-161, VF-41, VMFAT-101, VF-111, VMFA-314, VF-154,
Major modifications – upgraded to F-4N in 1975-76
Final fate – on display in the Naval Aviation Museum at NAS Pensacola, Florida

13

F-4B BuNo 153020/NF 100 of Lt Cdr Ronald E McKeown and Lt John C Ensch, VF-161, USS *Midway*, 23 May 1972
Delivered – 27 May 1966
Units served with – VF-121, VF-213, VF-114, VF-92, VMFA-314, VMFA-122, VF-161
Major modifications – none
Final fate – downed by a SAM and the crew forced to eject over Nam Dinh on 25 August 1972. Pilot killed and RIO captured

14

F-4B BuNo 149457/NL 113 of Lt Winston W Copeland and Lt Donald R Bouchoux, VF-51, USS *Coral Sea*, 11 June 1972
Delivered – 11 June 1962
Units served with – VF-121, VMF(AW)-314, VMFA-513, VMFA-542, VF-51, VF-21, VF-142, VF-143, VF-114, VMFA-122, VMFA-314, H&MS-33, H&MS-11, VMFA-531,
Major modifications – none
Final fate – currently in storage with the Naval Aviation Museum at NAS Pensacola, having previously been displayed in front of the nearby Naval Aviation Schools Command for many years

15

F-4B BuNo 149473/NL 114 of Cdr Foster S Teague and Lt Ralph M Howell, VF-161, USS *Midway*, 11 June 1972
Delivered – 25 July 1962
Units served with – VF-102, VF-101, VF-14, VF-31, VF-74, VF-32, VMFAT-201, VMFAT-101, H&MS-33, H&MS-11, VF-51, Naval Missile Center
Major modifications – none
Final fate – destroyed as a range target at Holloman AFB, New Mexico, in 1973-74

16

F-4J BuNo 157307/AC 106 of Cdr Samuel C Flynn and Lt William H John, VF-31, USS *Saratoga*, 21 June 1972
Delivered – 18 December 1970
Units served with – VF-31, VF-33, VF-103, VF-171, VMFAT-101, VMFA-232,
Major modifications – upgraded to F-4S in 1983
Final fate – currently on stored at the National Air and Space Museum's Dulles International Airport facility, Washington, DC

17

F-4J BuNo 157299/AC 206 of Lt Cdr Robert E Tucker, Jr and Lt(jg) Stanley B Edens, VF-103, USS *Saratoga*, 10 August 1972
Delivered – 24 November 1970
Units served with – VF-103, VF-11
Major modifications – none
Final fate – lost in a flying accident on 9 February 1977 whilst participating in a daytime ACM training sortie from Oceana, the aircraft suffering an in-flight fire within the fuselage. The crew ejected safely

18

F-4E 67-0239/ZF of Capt Lawrence G Richard USMC and Lt Cdr Michael J Ettel USN, 58th TFS/432nd TRW, Udorn RTAFB, Thailand, 12 August 1972
Delivered – May 1968
Units served with – 15th TFW, 560th TFS/4531st TFW, 308th TFS/31st TFW, 432nd TRW (TDY)
Major modifications – none
Final fate – supplied to the Egyptian air force as part of Operation *Peace Pharoah*, the jet is still in frontline service with the 222nd Tactical Fighter Brigade at Quahira-West air base

19

F-4J BuNo 155526/AJ 201 of Maj Lee T Lasseter and Capt John D Cummings, VMFA-333, USS *America*, 11 September 1972
Delivered – 8 February 1968
Units served with – VF-103, VMFA-333
Major modifications – none
Final fate – damaged by a SAM and the crew forced to eject over the Gulf of Tonkin on 11 September 1972

20

F-4J BuNo 155846/NK 212 of Lt(jg) Scott H Davis and Lt(jg) Geoffrey H Ulrich, VF-142, USS *Enterprise*, 28 December 1972
Delivered – 23 January 1969
Units served with – VF-121, VF-142,
Major modifications – none
Final fate – aircraft crashed at sea off South Vietnam on 3 May 1973 after its crew suffered severe control problems. Both men ejected safely

21

F-4B BuNo 153045/NF 102 of Lt Victor T Kovaleski and Lt(jg) James A Wise, VF-161, USS *Midway*, 12 January 1973
Delivered – 17 August 1966
Units served with – VF-101, VF-74, VF-114, VF-161, VF-301, H&MS-41, VMFA-112

Major modifications – upgraded to F-4N in 1974-75
Final fate – withdrawn from service in September
1983, the jet's final disposition remains unknown

COLOUR SECTION

1
VF-96 'MiG killer' BuNo 157267 poses with the San
Diego Aerospace Museum's MiG-17F (ex-Egyptian
air force) at the General Dynamics plant in San
Diego in October 1989. Five months later both jets
were mounted on poles within the atrium at the
museum in Balboa Park (*via Robert F Dorr*)

2
Matt Connelly and Tom Blonski's 'Showtime 106'
(BuNo 155769) formates with a second jet from
VF-96 in early 1972 (*via Peter Mersky*)

3
Steve Shoemaker and Keith Crenshaw's
'Showtime 111' was photographed on the Miramar
ramp in late 1971. Converted into a QF-4S target
drone, this aircraft was lost in a fatal crash at the
Point Mugu airshow in April 2002 (*via B Elward*)

4
Formerly 'Showtime 112', dual 'MiG-killing' F-4J
BuNo 157267 left VF-96 for VF-114 (via VF-121) in
late 1972, and served with the 'Aardvarks' until
April 1975 (*via Peter Mersky*)

5
'Linfield 201' (BuNo 157245) is seen with a
suitably-marked travel pod mounted beneath its
port wing. Photographed in 1971, this aircraft
claimed a MiG-21 on 6 May 1972 (*via A Romano*)

6
VF-92's full complement of aircrew pose for a
squadron photo in their 'Friday suits' whilst in the
Gulf of Tonkin in 1972. Providing the backdrop to
this shot is VF-92's CAG jet, BuNo 155799. All Navy
units have these unofficial flightsuits made up in
their squadron colours pre-cruise, but they are
worn only on training flights (*via Peter E Davies*)

7 & 8
Seen at Miramar in August 1972, weeks after
completing a gruelling Vietnam cruise, 'Screaming
Eagle 110' shows clear signs of fatigue. This jet
was used by Ken Cannon and Roy Morris to down
a MiG-17 on 10 May. Ironically, it was assigned to
Winston 'Mad Dog' Copeland (and his usual RIO
Dale Arends), who downed a MiG-17 on 11 June in
Cannon and Morris's 'Screaming Eagle 113' (BuNo
149457)! Wearing the modex 111 on cruise, the
F-4B features Copeland's name spelt incorrectly on
the canopy rail – it had been erroneously applied
with an 's' at the end (*via A Romano and B Elward*)

9
An unknown pilot and RIO Lt Steve Brainerd strap
into 'Rock River 110' (BuNo 153068) in August

1972. This aircraft had been used by 'Bart'
Bartholomay and Oran Brown to destroy a MiG-19
on 18 May 1972 – their names appear on the
canopy rails, and a kill marking is partially visible
at the base of the splitter vane (*M Padgett*)

10
'Rock River 101' runs up in full afterburner prior
to taking a 'cat shot' in mid 1972. Commenting
on the jet's 'patch painting on the vertical fin',
photographer Michael Padgett, who was VF-161's
Corrosion Control Supervisor for this cruise,
remembers 'Paint jobs were just maintained on
the "boat". Whole aircraft painting, or even large
section painting, was discouraged' (*M Padgett*)

11
The splitter plate kill markings applied to 'Mugs'
McKeown and Jack Ensch's 'Rock River 100'
(BuNo 153020) in the wake of their MiG-17 claims
on 23 May 1972. This jet was subsequently shot
down by a SAM on 25 August 1972 (*M Padgett*)

12
Wearing standard flightsuits, VF-161 aircrew pose
for a cruise book shot in April 1972. They had been
aboard CVA-41 just a matter of days when this
photo was taken (*Mike Rabb via Jack Ensch*)

13
Michael Padgett painted the tail markings on most
VF-161 jets in 1972, and he also decorated the door
to the unit's ready room (dubbed *The "ROCK'S"
Den*). 'I stood many a watch behind that door', he
remembers (*M Padgett*)

14
VF-51 'MiG killer' BuNo 149457 was photographed
in storage at NARF North Island on 13 November
1976. Assigned to the Naval Aviation Museum at
NAS Pensacola since the late 1970s, the jet is
presently in storage once again after having been
displayed in front of the nearby Naval Aviation
Schools Command for many years (*via R F Dorr*)

15
The assigned F-4J (BuNo 157293) of VF-31's Sam
Flynn and Bill John wore their MiG kill symbol,
although it was not a 'MiG killer' (*via B Elward*)

16
Three VMFA-333 F-4Js share the fantail on a rainy
CVA-66 with other jets from CVW-8 (*via B Elward*)

17
Sister-ship to VF-142 'MiG killer' BuNo 155846,
'Dakota 213' is seen at Miramar in June 1973
(*via B Elward*)

18
Scorer of the final aerial victory to be claimed by
an American aircraft in the Vietnam War, 'Rock
River 102' (BuNo 153045) rests on the Miramar
ramp in the spring of 1973 (*via A Romano*)

INDEX

References to illustrations are shown in **bold**. Colour plates and Colour Section illustrations are prefixed 'pl.' and 'cs.', with page and caption locators in brackets.